Presentation Strategies & Dialogues

Presentation

Strategies & Dialogues

Christina M. Scalise

Fairchild Books
New York

Executive Director & General Manager: Michael Schluter
Executive Editor: Olga T. Kontzias
Assistant Acquisitions Editor: Amanda Breccia
Senior Development Editor: Joseph Miranda
Development Editor: Sylvia L. Weber
Assistant Art Director: Sarah Silberg
Production Director: Ginger Hillman
Production Editor: Linda Feldman
Ancillaries Editor: Amy Butler
Associate Director of Sales: Melanie Sankel
Copy editor: Edwin Chapman
Cover Design: Ray Shappell
Text Design: Mike Suh
Page Layout: Susan Ramundo
Photo Research: Avital Aronowitz
Text Permissions: Sigali Hamberger
Illustrations: Vanessa Han

Library of Congress Catalog Card Number: 2011936305

ISBN: 978-1-60901-144-4
GST R 133004424
Printed in the United States of America
TP09

Dedication

For Dolores, my mother, muse, and enthusiast.
Thank you for your idyllic balance of creativity, comedy, and love.

Contents

Extended Contents

◄ **x** ►

Preface

As designers, we shape solutions. We also shape client reaction, in that design evokes emotion. Designers analyze design for objectives, and their thoughts, words, bodies, and spirits bring personality to the design presentation. The heart of this book, *Presentation Strategies and Dialogues*, addresses the delivery strategy of unveiling a design solution. The key objective is to empower designers with analytical and physical tools that allow them to use imagination, voice, gesture, presence, and visual content to unveil their solutions with confidence. The use of analogies between theater and design presentations emphasizes preparation and performing. Designers create the setting and props for a design presentation and act their part in the production.

This is a how-to book on presentation practices to be used by any design student as reference for a design studio class or as a textbook for professional practice courses.

Students will learn to:
- Develop the oral segments, including a concise opening message and a motivating summation; establish a sequence of presenting; adopt an individual flow; and discover ways to connect to the client as the viewer.
- Apply practical and engaging strategies to establish a clear statement of the project concept and its important features.
- Organize, prepare, and arrange materials in a logical sequence.

- Collaborate by anticipating objections and planning strategies for dealing with them; arriving at authorization to proceed; and closing with a course of action.
- Triumph over fear of presenting; to rehearse (including videotaping); to master timing; and to tackle preparatory tasks.

Additional topics include working with the physical presentation environment, setting up the primary elements of the presentation, and making the presentation to the client. Included are techniques on critiques, performance evaluation, follow-up responsibilities, and courtesies to the client. The final chapter content is about developing a personal presentation style, incorporating dimensions of flow, and making an influential impression. This chapter sets all previous chapters in an environment that shows consideration for both client and subject matter.

Each chapter includes an opening anecdote offering a practical experience from a professional to make the book personally reachable. The book is easy to read, and its short chapters are sequenced to guide students through the process. Illustrated examples, quotations, and advice from practicing interior design professionals and other experts regarding presentations appear throughout the chapters. Performance tips are included throughout the text with dialogues and margin notes. Strategies and skills presented are relevant to each phase of the design process and applicable to informal and formal interior design presentations and meetings.

Students are exposed to authentic, polished, and contemporary presentation method ideas at the end of each chapter. These are presented with select interview questions and answers with professional designers about their presentation style and related to instruction in the chapter. The interviews are used to affirm and enhance important subject matter or to initiate practice of skill development. *Idea Exchange* is an interactive exploration of presentation-related subject matter through discussion video and article links. Finally, *Create Experience* gives students an opportunity to build their skills through practice assignments in each chapter. Practice activities range from short exercises to lengthy projects for group and individual preparation. Experiences are developed to establish presentation styles and techniques.

The text addresses NCIDQ testing areas and CIDA standards that relate to professionalism in communicating design solutions to clients.

Acknowledgments

The curtain call in admiration and gratitude to the players:

Soliloquy: Massimo Vignelli, president of Vignelli Associates; Peter and Corinna Joehnk, principals at JOI Design; Vicente Wolf, Vicente Wolf Associates; John R. Sadlon, managing principal, and Alan Dandron, principal at Mancini Duffy; Tod Williams, Billie Tsien, and Octavia Giovannini-Torelli, TWBTA architects; Paul Conner, vice president of Behavioral Science, Sentient Decision Science Inc.; Marco Frascari; Paul Goldberger; José E. Solís Betancourt; Kazuyo Sejima and Ryue Nishizawa; Samuel Botero; Tony Chi; and Kristyn Hill.

Prompt and Cue: Ruth Stern and Gregory Hoffman.

Bard in the Wings: Tiffany Santos (artistic expression).

Claqueurs and Chorus: Mary Slater, Guy Romagna, MaryJo Capizzi, Bina Abling, Cheryl Kramer, Tony Scalise, and most of all my parents, Anthony and Dolores Scalise.

Director of Storytelling: Olga Kontzias, executive editor at Fairchild Books.

Deputy Stage Manager: Joseph Miranda, senior development editor at Fairchild Books.

Animateur: Sylvia Weber, development editor at Fairchild Books.

Props: Sarah Silberg, assistant art director at Fairchild Books; Avital Aronowitz, photo researcher; Sigali Hamberger, text permissions researcher.

Exposition: Amy Butler, ancillaries editor at Fairchild Books.

Technical Rehearsal: Linda Feldman, production editor at Fairchild Books.

Critics and Tritagonists: Holly L. Cline, Radford University; Ted Drab, Oklahoma State University; Elizabeth Dull, High Point University; Ellen McDowell, Art Institute of Pittsburgh; Sharran Parkinson, Virginia Commonwealth University; Susan Ray-Degges, North Dakota State University; and Erin Speck, George Washington University.

Bravo.

ACKNOWLEDGMENTS

Introduction

"The word 'design' comes from the Italian word *disegno*, and you might assume that that word derived from Latin, but in Latin there was no such word. Rather, the Italian word slowly arose within the field of architecture—not the other fine arts—and it was related to what was called 'designation' (*disegnare equals designare*). If you think about it, the designer is the one who 'designates' where things go. In the pre-Renaissance era, one might draw a 'plan' of a building by putting poles in spots designating the corners of the actual structure to be built. 'Design' was much more broadly understood to be a craft—an ongoing and circular process—than it is now, when it is generally associated with a finished object that may be regarded as a work of art. Gradually, the modern sense of the word emerged, and became understood as *l'arte del disegno*—the art of design."[1]
— Marco Frascari

Frascari is referring to linguistics to explain why analytical drawing is associated with Italy for its origins. Expressing design requires both analytical drawing and language to advance design communication. A simple string of words has **expressive power, and the focus of this book is using the language of the art of design**. In as few as five passionate sentences, some designers can convey information that gives months of work useful meaning to the client. Similarly, of course, five sentences are enough for a designer to cause immense uncertainty. Moreover, a disorganized, poorly prepared presentation inevitably leads to the assassination of a solid, well-crafted design solution. This slaughter can be prevented.

The unveiling of a design solution is comprehensive in scope. In order to deliver a successful talk, you must be organized, prepared, and enthusiastic about the entire project. Bruce Alberts shared these thoughts during an interview with Charlie Rose:

I think the important thing is that creativity is not making up things, using science, just in your head; you have to know a fair amount of information about different fields that are related and different ways of thinking about problem solving, and then make up your own solution . . . putting those pieces together.[2]

Putting those pieces together involves other design disciplines and incorporating the benefits of their contributions. You, related design professionals, and the client are collaborators.

The role of emotions in design experiences is important. Designers must understand their client both as the end user and as the viewer of a presentation. Emotion influences design, and a presentation is an intervention that influences emotion. Your visuals are your tools for communicating your vision; use them to reinforce the concept and structure of your presentation. Your language explains your reason for your vision; learn to speak the language of design to help define concepts and communicate your passion for your interior design solutions.

We forget that the highest objective of selling design is to spark the client's passion for the solution—to evoke an emotional response. This book provides analytical and physical techniques whereby the designer can bring the design story to life while demonstrating how the solution meets the client's objectives and needs.

"This is the gesture of the music. I'm opening a space for you to put in another layer of interpretation."
— Carlos Kleiber, conductor[3]

Presentation Strategies & Dialogues

1 The Language of Design

The true sign that the [New York] Times had got religion about architecture was the way Renzo Piano, and not one of the Times executives or public officials who were present, turned out to be the star of the show. Piano, who has a gray beard and never seems entirely comfortable in a business suit, speaks with a mellifluous Italian accent. Even though he was trained as an engineer, he is probably better than any [other] architect at convincing people that buildings are not just objects of shelter but exercises in poetry. For fifteen minutes, he held his audience rapt as he explained the rationale of the building, which is to be a slender tower of transparent glass, sheathed in a webbing of white ceramic rods that will form a protective sunscreen.

"For no reason, I prefer things that are light," Piano said, sauntering back and forth beside a set of renderings and floor plans on easels and a six-foot-high model of the building. "An architect fights all his life against gravity—this is our destiny, a building that is light and transparent and vibrant. It is like it is breathing, and it keeps changing. . . . Architecture is, of course, about making buildings, but it is also about telling stories, and the story I hope this building tells is not about arrogance and power. I hope this building will tell a story about transparency and lightness."

The outer mesh of ceramic would give the tower a soft texture and make it appear almost like mist against the sky. Piano said the rods would look like lace, and at one point, he spoke of his desire to juxtapose "the 'precarity' of the lace and the strength of the steel." He thought for a moment, and then turned to Michael Golden, the Times company's vice-chairman, and said, "Don't worry, Mike. The lace won't really be precarious."[1]

— Paul Goldberger, architecture critic for *The New Yorker*

The language used by Piano expressed his passion and, in turn, captured the imaginations of his viewers. Like Piano, Massimo Vignelli is a designer who is emotionally engaging when presenting. Both Vicente Wolf and Peter Joehnk relate that they are more emotional with the presentation than during the design process! Furthermore, the presentation offers the chance to weave the story of the design solution. The delightful storytelling of architectural critic Paul Goldberger is captivating for a reader. Interior design solutions do not sell on visuals alone. Consequently, a persuasive presentation allows the client or viewer to be emotionally involved with the project and motivated to buy. This chapter reveals storytelling strategies for design presentation, striking a balance between emotional connection and tangible results. During an oral presentation, the client focuses on what the designer is saying. This is a chance for the designer to articulate a sense of passion.

Expressing a Creative Thought

One of the most powerful ways of articulating passion is by harnessing the strength of narrative. Professionals enlighten the client with a narrative of how they arrived at the project solution. This entails relating how the aspects of the client's design problem were approached to best meet the client's needs. Design professionals talk about and point out the special features of the solution. They know how to demonstrate to the client that their design solution reflects the project guidelines and the needs and requests of the client and that it supports the strategy or design concept. The presentation must be carefully prepared and must explore and analyze the design project. This effort by the designer is in addition to the hard work of addressing the challenges of the project and preparing the visuals of the presentation.

When crafting your narrative, be sure to pay attention to word choice. *Sophisticated. Pearl. Precious.* These are truthful, subtle words

to motivate a client to say yes. These are expressions used by Stefano Giovannoni to describe white mosaic tile. Reflect on his language with respect to a color and material choice:

> We decided to use mosaic. In this case, we chose white mosaic. I think that it is an exceptional material [because of] its extremely sophisticated texture: Its surface is perceived as homogeneous, but inside there's a whole variety of tiny reflections and refractions of mother-of-pearl color that make it very precious and interesting.[2]

This persuasive description creates a strong connection and engagement with the material. It evokes an emotional experience of the material's qualities instead of merely identifying it as white mosaic.

Once you know what features you plan to emphasize, you have to decide how to do so. Expressing the creative thought process is a way of translating visual characteristics. When you translate the visual characteristics of a design, you use words to express your creative thought process.

The expression can be humorous, personal, daring, eccentric, or entertaining. It should affirm your informed experience of the client and design. A knowledgeable familiarity with clients includes their individuality, needs, and work or living culture. Your informed experience of design includes interior design history, theory, and process. These aspects of design experience are your design vocabulary of expression.

At the same time, we add more words to the vocabulary range in Figure 1.1 to describe or modify the design features to develop a presentation design language. Piano spoke of the illusion of a "soft texture"; likewise, texture could be reflective and smooth. It is your decision regarding how to emphasize the visual characteristics of your design. This is your opportunity to set standards against which the client can evaluate the content of the proposed design and then justify the associated expense. Your responsibility is to tell the truth about what you see and why

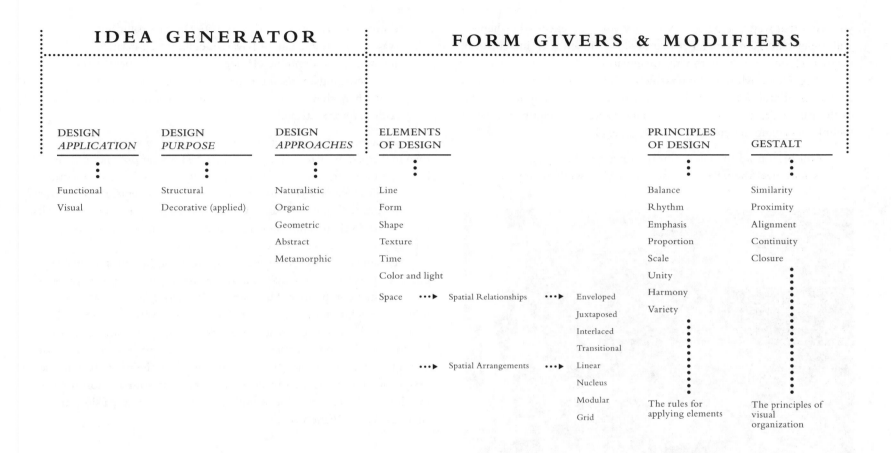

IDEA GENERATOR

FORM GIVERS & MODIFIERS

DESIGN *APPLICATION*	DESIGN *PURPOSE*	DESIGN *APPROACHES*	ELEMENTS OF DESIGN			PRINCIPLES OF DESIGN	GESTALT
Functional	Structural	Naturalistic	Line			Balance	Similarity
Visual	Decorative (applied)	Organic	Form			Rhythm	Proximity
		Geometric	Shape			Emphasis	Alignment
		Abstract	Texture			Proportion	Continuity
		Metamorphic	Time			Scale	Closure
			Color and light			Unity	
			Space ••▶	Spatial Relationships ••▶	Enveloped	Harmony	
					Juxtaposed	Variety	
					Interlaced		
					Transitional		
			••▶	Spatial Arrangements ••▶	Linear		
					Nucleus		
					Modular	The rules for applying elements	The principles of visual organization
					Grid		

◀ **5** ▶

Figure 1.1
Design language creates a design composition as well as describing characteristics of a design composition. For instance, Gestalt theory, design approach, and elements and principles of design all have unique expressions. Each has its own language, including words like alignment, continuity, juxtapose, balance, rhythm, form, line, color, and texture, to name a few.

you see it that way. Use design vocabulary your audience—the client—will understand. Also remember that design is linked with imagination; for that reason, describe with your imagination.

The Dolce Munich Unterschleissheim is a modern conference center and hotel that uniquely weaves together a contemporary tale of Bavarian culture with the Dolce brand values. See Figure 1.2. Peter Joehnk, managing director of JOI-Design, explains:

> Our brief from the client was to conceive a hotel that would meet the needs of business travelers while telling

Figure 1.2
Dolce Hotels and Resorts, designed by JOI-Design, defines its brand identity through the concepts of "nourishment" (nurturing the spirit, mind, and body of its guests), "connectivity" (delivering environments that bring people together and promote thoughtful exchange), and "community" (offering customer service and environmentally responsible business practices that benefits each guest). *(Peter Joehnk, principal at JOI-Design, interview by Christina Scalise, electronic questionnaire, June 18, 2010)*

a story through its individuality. JOI-Design's solution was to construct a tale of Bavarian culture that balances masculine and feminine elements across its schemes while creating an *island* for the guests—an inclusive setting where their desires for *nourishment, connectivity* and *community* are satisfied.[3]

Expression and interaction are complex in modern times, more so than in the past. In determining the language for your presentation, finding ways to engage an inquisitive client without insulting an informed one is your challenge. Become familiar with your clients. Prepare your presentation with them in mind. Carefully organize it in a way that will make sense to them, and use language they will understand. Skimping on this preparation will not serve your purpose.

Designers must be sophisticated speakers of their professional language to persuade clients to sign, to win their emotional support—in short, to stay competitive. The language of design is the technique of using your skills and knowledge to inform creatively (see Figure 1.3). You speak this language to sell your ideas so they do not figuratively breathe their last in the presentation. The practical purpose of the design presentation is to persuade the client to authorize the next phase in the design process. A higher objective is to transmit your passion for the solution to the client. Achieve both goals by triggering passion in the client as Renzo Piano does.

▶ The preliminary concept drawings prepared in the ideation phase of design convey a host of features and solutions. They help to reconnect with that phase when developing a presentation dialogue. Access the creative part of your brain again and recapture a feel for the character of the space, using your early imagery.

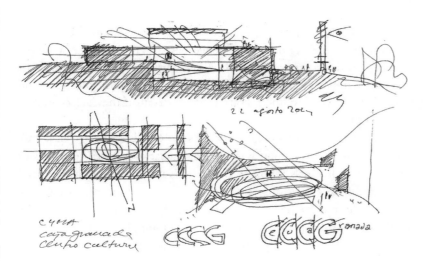

Figure 1.3
The description of this design concept using design language: the plan is a geometric composition, and the design demonstrates the use of radial balance. *(Concept studies of the Museo de Andalucia, Granada, Spain. Alberto Campo Baeza, Architect)*

Storytelling

Designers use drawings, images, and words to explain concepts and give features verve when describing the aesthetics and function of a project. When presenting your design, you can be pragmatic with the use of facts, statistics, and the practical aspects of the design solution; nevertheless, a more lively approach applies descriptions, metaphors or analogies, anecdotes, examples, and personalization. In combination, these are effective strategies to inform and hold the attention of the viewers as well as win their support or approval.

Basically, when preparing your presentation the choice is between simply telling and creative storytelling. You can show where the materials are applied in a space—point and tell—or you can describe why the materials are the right choice for the space. For example, you can merely point to a space on the plan and say, "This is the lobby"—point and tell—or you can say, "The lobby is the collective stage for social interaction, centrally located, in this public zone." The description of the lobby as a "collective stage" has vivaciousness, and the term "social interaction" points to the function of the space as alive. When this description is woven together for the client, it creates an overall experience, as in storytelling.

Several fundamental strategies used to develop persuasive narration for the design details follow. Let's review a few statements as examples for each style:

Practical

Define the useful or functional purposes. Point out such features:

- "Technical conveniences (or acoustical demands) are the essentials of the design approach."
- "The stainless steel legs of the chairs are fastened to the floor to facilitate maintenance of the travertine floor."
- "This material (define material) insulates both walls and ceilings."
- "The window covering cuts down on glare and heat."
- "The movable partitions provide flexibility of use."

Some clients favor the to-the-point style of presentations and prefer not to be sold. It is an expedient path to approval; however, it is tedious for the listener. When you know your audience, you will know when and how to use this style.

Factual and Statistical

Present concise, factual information rather than an interpretation of information. Any information that is verifiable data is factual. Statistical data is the use of numerical data relating to the problem. For example:

- "This carpet has biodegradable fibers and dyes. A number to call for free recycling is available, creating a "Cradle-to-Cradle" manufacturing, distribution, and reuse cycle."[4]
- "Currently the space is 2,100 square feet, and we have increased it to 2,400 square feet. By rearranging the plan layout and combining storage areas, we gained the extra space. By using modular system furniture, we have increased the number of workstations by 15 percent."
- "The upholstery textile has the Class A Heavy Duty rating for abrasion. It is very suitable for commercial use in terms of durability."
- Cite evidence-based design (EBD) research statistics to support your solution. A health care client may expect this type of information.

In the above examples, define terms "Cradle-to-Cradle," Class A Heavy Duty, and EBD for the client, if necessary, because they are examples of industry-specific language. Designers educate their clients while at the same time showing respect for their listeners' ability to understand the story behind the design. Clients make decisions based on the information provided in the presentation. A true professional and expert of interior design is attentive to where and when to use industry-specific language and when more definition is needed for the client. Refer to Chapter 3 for a discussion of adapting your use of professional terminology to your clients' familiarity with the vocabulary.

Other facts include features such as product warranties, maintenance, code compliance, Leadership in Energy and Environmental Design (LEED) certification, energy efficiency, Reveal rating, and so on. Discuss programming data or evidence-based design criteria or simply identify on drawings with notations. Use statistical data, on its own or to make comparisons, only if it is significant to the project criteria and supportive of your solution. Narrate these details if they are central to the client's perception.

Rather than encouraging attention to details only specialists care about, focus on explaining why you did what you did. The ranges of end users, individuals who use the design, are not simply categorized by digits; therefore, do not use only quantitative data. Insight and understanding into the needs and aspirations of end users comes from the qualitative data, and you present ideas using multiple methods.

Descriptive

Inform by describing the characteristics of your design, using details to appeal to the senses. Captivate the client's emotional, physical, and intellectual sensibilities with enriching and vivid details. When communicating the design, use active verbs and precise modifiers. Use statements like the following:

- "The square became our basic unit of color and pattern by juxtaposing a wide range of hues within a very limited color palette (referring to yarn dyes)."[5] This statement reveals the use of design theory in utilizing a geometric approach modified with color, texture, and pattern.
- "Despite the simple rectangular floor plan of the house, spaces merge into each other with a minimal use of partitions . . . a light freestanding staircase with a minimalist railing hanging from the ceiling is glass walled on one side . . . floor-to-ceiling windows frame the cityscape; all these architectural elements emphasize the idea of uninterrupted space."[6]

Think about why you made each of your design decisions, and it will be easier to describe the particular feature. The descriptive words are especially important to include when design elements are not evident on the drawings, a client does not or cannot understand drawings, or the benefit is significant for the end user. Universal design solutions, for example, the texture, form, and size of a handrail, have significant benefit for the end user: allowing a power grip, with all fingers and thumb able to curl around the handrail, regardless of the direction of the hand's approach to the handrail. "Verbal language is used in description where explanation goes hand-in-hand with the creative process, forcing invention where detail is lacking and expressing relationships not obvious visually."[7] In other words, if the form or shape of a handrail is not clearly defined by a design drawing such as an elevation, describe those features and benefits.

Anecdote

Describe with a short related story that could be a remarkable, amusing, positive, or negative experience to call attention to features.

> Honoré de Balzac lived many years in a cold and all but empty attic. There was no flame in his fireplace, no picture on his wall. But on one wall he inscribed with charcoal: "Rosewood paneling with commode." On another, "Gobelin tapestry with Venetian mirror," and in the place of honor over the fireless grate, "Picture by Raphael."[8]
> —Honoré de Balzac (1799–1850), French novelist

The Balzac anecdote is an amusing prologue to create storytelling for a client's first home. You can follow the anecdote with descriptions of the special features on their walls and fireplace. Remember that anecdotes may not be hard data, but at the same time, observational research situations can have significant importance. Use them to introduce, illustrate, or emphasize your relevant point. Designers have many experiences from which to draw. Indeed, anecdotes from or about professional designers are used as chapter openings in this book. Students can collect stories by observing, reading, researching, and inquiring. When you recount an anecdote from others, be sure to give an accurate attribution. Be discreet when sharing the stories by protecting a name or company if the story is not public knowledge. In some cases, "it is essential to protect the identity and privacy of individuals, companies, and even circumstances."[9] Frank Gehry does this in telling the Frank Lloyd Wright story by not mentioning the client's name or project.

> ▶ "You've all heard the Frank Lloyd Wright story, when the woman called and said, 'Mr. Wright, I'm sitting on the couch, and the water's pouring in on my head.' And he said, 'Madam, move your chair.' " Anecdote shared by Frank Gehry, Architect, with Richard Saul Wurman.

Example

Illustrate your point with a specific instance, as in these examples:

- "The Reading Room 2020 collaborative environment by Philips is intuitive and as simple to use as your iPhone. The collaboration table/desktop surface is similar to the iPhone Multi-touch Display. Let's look at this video to show you how swift interaction with colleagues can be." (The designer opens this link for the client to play the video: www.design .philips.com/philips/sites/philipsdesign/about/design/design-portfolio/design_futures/reading_room_2020.page.) Ambient Experience is a purposefully designed environment that makes patients and employees feel more comfortable.

"After our site visits, meetings, and initial research regarding your health-care environments, we believe you will benefit by starting or participating in a design approach such as the SPARC[10] Program at the Mayo Clinic. SPARC is involved with finding new solutions through observational research and prototyping, focusing on how to make the experience of being a patient better."

You may find it useful to discuss how other companies are using a product or solution. Of course, the material samples and graphic illustrations are the primary way that designers use very specific examples to reveal the solution to the client.

Include, Implicate, or Personalize

Apply your solution exclusively to the client. In these examples, the designer points out that:

- "We studied the communication patterns within your departments and discovered a need for a place to connect for individual project team meetings on a daily basis. We solved it for you by including three team meeting spaces centrally located between the departments. It will dramatically improve project communications."
- "This design concept solution complements your brand personality and fits like a glove." (Explain how it does this.)
- "From what you have told us about the profile of your customer, the concept for your space is developed around the theme of journey."
- "You love French antiques. With that in mind, we found an heirloom of high value and quality for your foyer. You and your children will pass this fine demilune table down through generations."

Clearly, the creation of an interior is brought about through personalization because it is a custom design solution. Look for connections that may not be as obvious as well. This can also include describing the experience of the space. A bank is designed around a practical customer experience. Figure 1.4 is an experience of human perception.

Analogy and Metaphor

Imply a comparison between dissimilar objects or ideas. The comparison between Reading Room 2020 and an iPhone Multi-touch Display is a literal analogy. Many design concepts are ideas generated from metaphors or symbolism.

Figure 1.4
Vertigo Exhibit. The Berlin design studio Beta Tank's black-and-white, op-art-patterned installation features large inflatable balls that roll and bounce and optical illusions that pose questions about human perception—what is "real" and what isn't. (New York Times Style Magazine Design Blog; "Milan Report: Design Vertigo," blog entry by Pilar Viladas, April 14, 2010, http://tmagazine.blogs.nytimes.com/2010/04/14/milan-report-design-vertigo/.)

Jump Associates, a business strategy firm, designed its workplace to encourage an environment for collaborative teamwork around connection by using figurative analogies. The open and flexible spaces are *Neighborhoods* where the furniture can flow freely. The project rooms, named *Clubhouses*, include an entrance referred to as the *Front Porch*. The *Front Porch* spaces become the vehicle to solicit feedback posted with diagrams, notes, or thoughts about a current team project. *Zen Rooms* with low tables and pillows on the floor provide space for reflection and quiet creativity.

Spanish hotelier Antonio Pérez Navarro applies the metaphors of connection, resource, and journey in his hotel concepts. "Historic palaces and other buildings offer a connection to the past. Restful sleep is the factory of your energy for tomorrow, but it's also the factory of your dreams for the future,"[11] Navarro suggests.

Consequently, use narratives to stimulate design thinking and develop the confidence to express your design concepts. When you recount the process of solving the design problem, you invite the viewer to participate in the design story. Well-designed concepts are alluring and charismatic in addition to purposeful. The end user and basic design theory are at the heart of both. In your statements, identify the client's problem, provide a solution, and reveal its benefits. Research and develop oral skills by reading books, trade magazines, product descriptions, white papers, and observing others. Be sure to explain any unfamiliar terms. It is central to begin your story early in the project and interlace the ideas throughout all of the elements of the design solution.

Deep Metaphors

Butterflies represent transformation. Transformation in the physical and emotional form influences hospital experiences, for example. Butterflies and the transformation theme are prominent in multiple areas of Children's Hospital of Pittsburgh. The simple metaphors used to describe design tap into the deeper metaphors, and several metaphors can imply one single metaphor. They are unlike the surface metaphors that we use in everyday speech such as "fits like a glove." Steven Pinker calls these dead metaphors because they are cliché. On the other hand, universal deep metaphors drive perception, and hence, behavior, say Harvard scholar Gerald Zaltman and his business collaborator, Lindsay Zaltman. These deep metaphors explain deep perceptions and needs: balance, transformation, journey, container, connection, resource, and control. When used to develop and present your concepts, these metaphors can result in effective solutions and responses.

One example of this use of deep metaphor is the Mondrian Hotel in South Beach, Florida; as visualized by Marcel Wanders, it is Sleeping Beauty's Castle. Owned by Morgans Hotel Group, the hotel is one of its many modern developments that incorporate fantasy and unpredictability into the design concepts. Wanders, well known for designing with humor and fantasy, hopes that designers realize they can be "beautiful poets." Morgans defines its collective legacy to "demonstrate the richest sense of daring, free thinking, and style . . ."[12] Sleeping Beauty evokes sleep, dreams, fantasy, fairy tales, escape, transformation, and journey. A similar metaphor concept mingles through the design of Maison Moschino as shown in Figure 1.5.

As we respond to the physical environment surrounding us, a change occurs in our state of mind. For example, think of a window as a symbol and reflect on what it represents to you. As designers, we use windows to illuminate a space or make it more expansive. We often describe it as letting in the natural light. For some, who cannot wait until the work week ends on Friday, in a work environment a window can also "let people out." A glass wall or expansive space such as an airport terminal can make one feel part of a larger container or not trapped. This terminal is a container for an emotional getaway. The experience of a transportation facility could be a metaphor of journey, transformation,

Figure 1.5
Life is a bed of roses. This hotel concept is an emotional getaway. *(Maison Moschino, Milan, Italy)*

connection, or balance depending on the diverse emotional needs of individuals. Homes, theaters, and shops can also be metaphors for these things. All buildings are physical containers.

Additionally, positive emotional metaphors, when appropriately aligned with a product, enhance interest in purchasing. For instance, the primary positive emotion experienced when purchasing home products is contentment, followed by control, and finally pride. The primary positive emotion experienced when purchasing products on display in public is pride, followed by control, and finally contentment. Remarkably, the same is true when purchasing clothing. When purchases are made for lounging around the house, contentment is the positive emotion. When purchasing clothing for going out, pride is the positive emotion. In brief, "pride enhanced the desire for products particularly useful for public" displays to "draw positive attention to oneself."[13] Contentment "enhanced the desire for products used in safe, familiar, and comfortable places, such as one's home."[14] Paul Conner of Emotive Analytics sums it up this way, "The point is that sometimes marketers or designers make the mistake of just making someone feel generally 'good' about their product or service without paying close attention to the specific kind of good they should be making people feel."[15]

Think like Renzo Piano who, for the Times Headquarters, also designed and insisted on a garden including trees and a towering central mast. Piano said of the mast, "it gives you something to love." Think like Steelcase—it sells solutions to enhance efficiency and the experience of workplaces, not simply furniture. It is instructive as well as inspiring to explore narrations by designers about the characteristics of their work. This includes expanding your world vision and investigating all of the

▶ Don't get precious about your work. At the same time, don't be afraid to push your ideas if you really think they will work.

arts. Think like an artist and contemplate this concept. A solution for the set design of *Cinderella*, Les Ballets de Monte-Carlo, is shown in Figures 1.6 and 1.7. The symbolism is revealed in this narrative by the artist and designer, Ernest Pignon-Ernest:

> For Jean-Christophe Maillot's *Romeo and Juliet*, I had already decided upon simplicity. For *Cinderella*, it was a light plastic concept, which was also called for. A very simple symbol for open scenery: the book, the support, the work itself, ready to be written throughout the ballet. For this book operates as a notebook, sketches withdrawn as soon as they are outlined, so as not to freeze the onlooker's imagination.[16]

Figure 1.6
A book concept is the scenery for the ballet and the blank pages of the book surround the dancers. Images and lighting are projected on the pages to create different atmospheres. *(Cendrillon. Jean-Christophe Maillot. Bernice Coppieters. © Photo Hans Gerritsen)*

Figure 1.7
"A picture book: twenty curved pages—an aluminum sheet 2mm thick—has the fluidity, the flexibility of paper, and upon which atmospheres, suggestions, notes almost, will be read in projection." *(Cendrillon. Jean-Christophe Maillot. Paola Cantalupo and Chris Roelandt. © Photo Hans Gerritsen. Pignon-Ernest, Ernest, "Cinderella: The scenery; a picture book," Les Ballets de Monte-Carlo, [April 3, 1999], http://www.balletsdemontecarlo.com/programmes_en/synopsis /cendrillon.html)*

By now, the concept begins to take you in the direction of a modern fairytale. The designer is also an artist who envisioned images using collage, watercolor, or pastels. He equates his technique to color strokes or simply suggesting images derived from his memories and perspectives. At this point, Pignon-Ernest rewrites the minimalist book pages with traditional elements. He described details such as a palatial Russian crystal chandelier, elements from a palace in Yemen, and draped garment pieces in a sixteenth-century painting to suggest the ballroom scene in the prince's palace. This description is magical. It invokes nuance with a few pieces of high-quality information. It plants a feeling in our minds.

Dialogue with Peter Joehnk

JOI-Design, Hamburg, Germany
Peter Joehnk, and Corinna Kretschmar-Joehnk, Principals

Q. What are the most exhilarating aspects of a design presentation?

A. When the client applauds and extends congratulations after the presentation is over.

Q. Do you have an interesting or humorous anecdote regarding a memorable design presentation experience?

A. Some time ago, I was making a presentation to a very wealthy client who was building a complex including two hotels, a theater, shops, and restaurants. A while into the presentation, I noticed the face of the client was getting very red and continued to get more red as I presented. Suddenly he shouted, "Squared architects shit," jumped up and left the room. Somehow we remained friends and have since done many projects together.[17]

Idea Exchange

- Ideation. Investigate how design professionals explain their concepts. Go to the Bisazza website, www.bisazza.com. Click on the "Designers" link and then browse through the designers' videos.
- Watch the video "Douglas Birkenshaw at IDS09—Interior Design Show, 2009" and explain the concept of Vertebrae, a seating station (http://www.di.net/videos/2991/).
- Watch the videos of hoteliers defining their concepts at Design Hotels: Made by Originals at www.designhotels.com/made_by_originals.
- Watch the Interview with Marcel Wanders on the Mondrian South Beach: www.youtube.com/watch?v=-pvoCmUnsYA&NR=1.

Create Experience

Discussion

Improvisation. Explore Figure 1.3 to gain experience with expressing a creative thought process. Answer these possible but unusual questions quickly and intuitively:

> What color is like this space?
>
> What season is like this space?
>
> Is there a piece of music that represents this space?
>
> Where is the focus of energy?
>
> Does the space move in straight lines or curves, and does it move quickly or slowly?
>
> Is it strong or light?
>
> What does the space reveal to you?
>
> What is the natural sequence of moving through the space?
>
> Where do the characteristics change?

You can add your own questions.

Engage. Repeat the Improvisation exercise using your own preliminary drawings. Think about metaphors to capture interest. Remember that clients do not have the same emotional connection to the project you do. Think of ways to make the connection for your client. To engage the client, do not merely identify the features of the solution; give them character.

2 Entice, Engage, Energize, and Equate

*J*osé E. Solís Betancourt suggests that designing a residence is like designing a set for an opera. "You create this amazing backdrop where clients can perform their lives," he says. "A space is like a procession of acts in a client's libretto." And, as with opera, he adds, "there are so many layers to it."[1]

— *Architectural Digest*

A presentation encapsulates an experience of the interior and can serve as a way to move the client through the procession of acts the space may hold. Therefore, you must identify the meaningful experiences in the design of the space and turn them into opportunities. This chapter is a basic itinerary that you can expand with the layers of richness and stimulation that describe your design solution. It is a dangerous idea to just show up with your visuals and wing the presentation (Figure 2.1). Carefully sequence your presentation in advance to guide the viewer. This chapter includes practical actions for the oral delivery presentation sequence as Figure 2.2 shows. Develop your itinerary for the presentation around these four segments: *Entice, Engage, Energize,* and *Equate.*

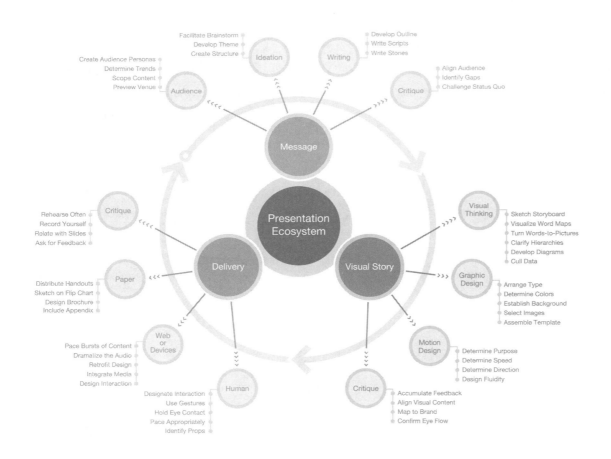

Figure 2.1
Presentation Ecosystem as presented by Nancy Duarte, Duarte Design, Mountain View, CA. Following a structure helps you organize and prepare the information you wish to communicate. A skillful presenter writes an overview or outline of the presentation detailing what to include, in what order, and how long to spend on each subject.

STORYTELLING

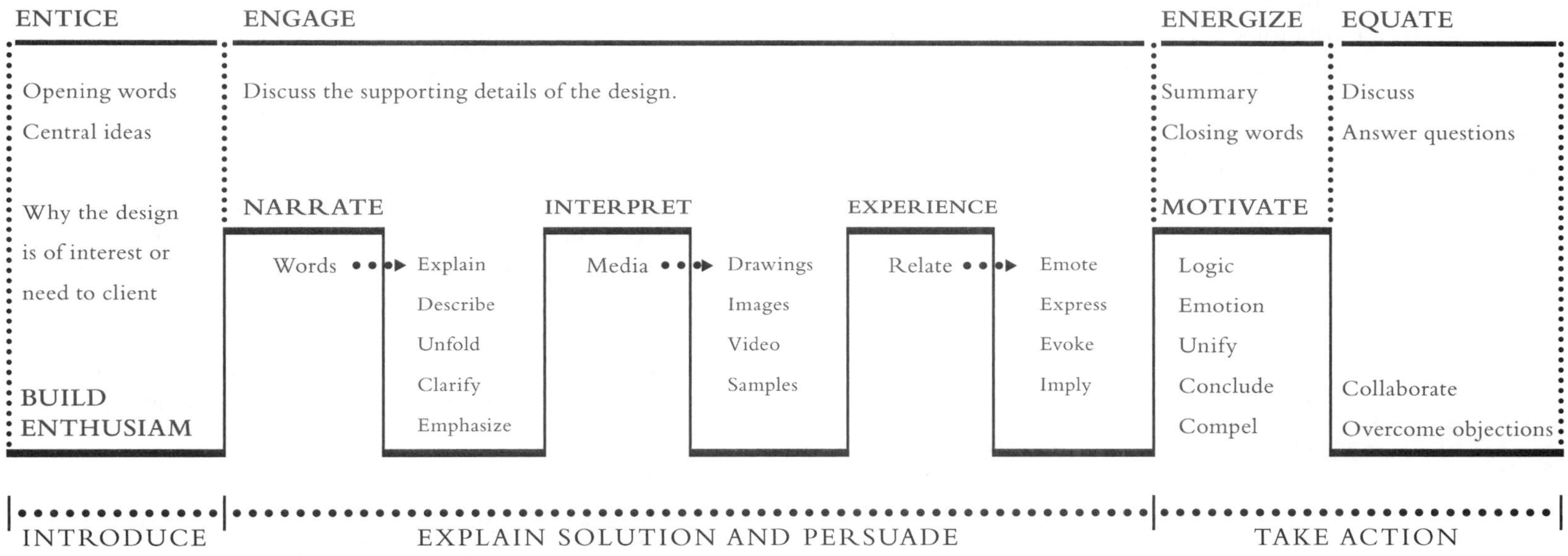

ENTICE	ENGAGE			ENERGIZE	EQUATE

ENTICE	ENGAGE	ENERGIZE	EQUATE
Opening words	Discuss the supporting details of the design.	Summary	Discuss
Central ideas		Closing words	Answer questions

	NARRATE	INTERPRET	EXPERIENCE	MOTIVATE	
Why the design is of interest or need to client	Words ●●●▶ Explain	Media ●●●▶ Drawings	Relate ●●●▶ Emote	Logic	
	Describe	Images	Express	Emotion	
	Unfold	Video	Evoke	Unify	
	Clarify	Samples	Imply	Conclude	Collaborate
BUILD ENTHUSIAM	Emphasize			Compel	Overcome objections

INTRODUCE	EXPLAIN SOLUTION AND PERSUADE	TAKE ACTION

Figure 2.2
Entice, *Engage*, *Energize*, and *Equate* segments. A clear explanation helps to convince the client of the choices you made during the design process. The opening ought to capture the interest of the client instantly, as well as make your passion contagious. Will you be presenting novel concepts to this audience or building on their prior knowledge? Either way, make sure you cover the basics clearly and early to avoid losing your audience.

Entice

Who can resist a well-crafted opening statement that enthusiastically conveys background information about a design? This prelude describes what you set out to do and gives some idea of the context, purpose, and overall concept of your design. It is also the place for you to clarify expectations and address those expectations. Kazuyo Sejima and Ryue Nishizawa of SANAA explained their design intention for the New Museum of Contemporary Art in New York City, as shown in Figure 2.3, this way:

> We have tried to design a transparent building in the sense that we are not hiding what is happening behind the surface of the structure. . . . The solution emerged

Figure 2.3
Museum models of the New Museum of Contemporary Art by SANNA.

through an extensive period of trial and error. We made numerous study models. . . . First, we arrived at the notion of the boxes themselves; each one represents a specific piece of the program developed by the museum. Then we tried shifting the boxes to render the inside of the building more accommodating and open, with more possibilities for daylight to enter spaces and views to appear at various points in the interiors.[2]

This is discovery. The narrative invites you to pick up the boxes and start shifting them around in your imagination. It gives a lasting impression because it reveals the story behind the design. Discovery becomes a memorable moment for viewers. The opening statements are the synthesis of your central concept or a preview of the content of the design presentation. It will set the mood for what is to follow and intensify the interest of the viewers. Let's discuss how to achieve a strong opening.

> ▶ Avoid obvious remarks such as "Hello, my name is . . ." The client already knows who you are and will introduce you to the other meeting participants before you begin your presentation. "Thank you" is always appropriate and gracious.

Thought Processes

Some designers use reason, or emotion, or a combination of the two. The benefits are a deeper understanding of the thought process that leads to support for the design concept and program. Taking the viewer through the process, strategies, and directions you took in finding a solution prepares them to move on to the solution you are presenting. Alan Dandron, principal of Mancini Duffy, advises:

It's always best to start with the big picture. For every project, the discovery process results in the creation of a Statement of Strategic Intent (SoSI). We use this statement to help focus and frame all of our presentations. We recap the goals of the SoSI and then walk through how the design responds to these goals. The agenda for the presentation usually goes in the following order:

- Review project goals
- Review big-picture concept
- Review specific features [of the design] and how they respond to the project goals.[3]

Dandron points out the importance of restating the goals early during the presentation and tying all aspects of the presentation to the goals.

Branding

Branding is another building block used to link the presentation elements together. What are the clusters of attributes associated with the client's brand? Continue those viewpoints into the design presentation opening if they drove the concept of the design. Attributes that find expression in architectural branding to define the corporate culture are often metaphors. For instance, Herman Miller presented a white paper (a type of research report or article), "Three-Dimensional Branding: Using Space as a Medium for the Message," exploring the associations of *Society and Community Orientation*, *Visual Quality*, *Innovation*, *Concern for Customers*, *Presence and Success*, and *Collaboration*. The report goes on to explain that selling the experience includes the creation of a fundamental premise that "engages the senses and leaves a distinct impression."[4] The cumulative result is a captivating storyline for the experience economy that has taken root over the past decade in businesses other than those selling entertainment. The shift from functional emphasis to emotional emphasis transformed business during the late twentieth century. Focus is on the importance of an individual or organization's need to attract customers and employees and portray a positive reputation to the community. B. Joseph Pine II and James H. Gilmore explain:

> Experiences are inherently personal, existing only in the mind of an individual who has been engaged on an emotional, physical, intellectual, or even spiritual level. Thus, no two people can have the same experience, because each experience derives from the interaction between the . . . event . . . and the individual's state of mind.[5]

Place the experience of the interior at the heart of the presentation as it has the true power to engage the client in a personal and memorable way.

▶ "Light lines, light spheres, light cubes—objects clearly defined in terms of geometry, which can be used flexibly according to the principle of modularity: this ensures new lighting units that are matched to the respective room situation every time. An interplay of brightness, shadow and colours—dynamic tools for interiors that address people's emotions." Matteo Thun, 2008, on the Sconfine luminaires manufactured by Zumtobel

Concept Statements

Concept statements are another valuable reference for an opening. They capture the essence of the project strategy. Design concept statement development is defined with three parts, as Figure 2.4 illustrates.

COMPONENTS OF A DESIGN CONCEPT STATEMENT

VISION RESULTING IN PROPOSED CONCEPT	APPROACH TO ACHIEVE RESULTS
Idea Generator	Form Giver
to evoke a sophisticated silk dress or scarf from the Neiman Marcus couture line.	*billowing in the coastal breezes of New England.*
	Application
	the form creates large bellows for the entry and signage, and then condenses the folds to create a dramatic image. The colors of the metal are timeless. The pattern follows the form and enhances moments within the building.

Figure 2.4
Kilmer states, "the concept statement establishes the underlying principles that the physical designs will address and should be written in simple, declarative sentences." Neiman Marcus, Natick, Massachusetts by Elkus Manfredi Architects. *(Kilmer, Rosemary and W. Otie Kilmer,* Designing Interiors. *[Fort Worth: Harcourt Brace Jovanovich College Publishers 1992], 167)*

Pierluigi Serraino captured the essence of each design with his narrations of architectural photographs by Julius Schulman. Although the projects date back to early modernism, they are as relevant now as they were innovative at that time. Here is an example from the book,

Julius Schulman: Modernism Rediscovered, of brief sentences relating to a design concept statement:

> The design scheme expresses elements to give emphasis to the idea of uninterrupted space and flexibility of use. Landscaping was central to the organization of the interior as a transitional device to connect the distinct spatial areas and creating a connection with the natural environment as well. The materials echo this same idea of merging the interior and exterior.[6]

Gabellini Sheppard Associates describes the concept for the Vera Wang Boutique in Manhattan's Soho district as a theater performance. If you were presenting this design, you might say:

> The new Vera Wang Boutique . . . reflects and extends the designer's sensibility of elegant, performative luxury. The 2,000 square-foot, two-level environment is infused with light and based on the dynamic qualities of a white box theater, an infinitely changeable space that shapes a variety of narratives.[7]

This storyline is guiding the experience and action within the space. The design is formulated around the idea of fashion as theater, and every detail takes you on the adventure (Figure 2.5).

Another example shown in Figure 2.6 is the conceptualization of the Princi Bakery in the heart of Milan by Claudio Silvestrin Architects: This project offers a new experience to the Milanese; a bread baked with organic flour, but without yeast, in a solid brick fire oven positioned in the bakery shop itself. A simple expanse of clear glass is all that separates the customers from the baking process, protecting them from the considerable heat of the exposed fire.[8] Silvestrin, like Gabellini,

Figure 2.5
Vera Wang Boutique by Gabellini Sheppard Associates. "The design comprises three main areas: the storefront area, considered as a proscenium stage, followed by the middle-stage main collection, and continuing with the backstage collection and changing areas. Customers enter as performers on a stage, stepping onto the elevated, double-height proscenium at the front of the store. The spatial sequence unfolds . . ." *(Photography by Paul Warchol. Gabellini Sheppard, "Vera Wang Boutique," Gabellini Sheppard Associates, accessed April 30, 2010. www.gabellinisheppard.com/index.php/Projects/retail/vera-wang-boutique-5h.html)*

Figure 2.6
Princi Bakery by Silvestrin Architects. The elements that are involved in the making of bread—water, air, earth, and fire—are strongly present in this work of rigorous geometry and pure, natural minerals. *(Photo © Matteo Piazza)*

also sets up a relationship of parts and emphasized the link between the product and the design materials and features.

Linking design and conceptual elements for the client is potentially a challenge, but also an opportunity. Again, we can take an example from the entertainment industry, which historically capitalized on the concept of experience design and adventure. Todd-Avery Lenahan of

ABA Design Studio expressed his concept for the Las Vegas Encore hotel as a state of mind. Note the comparison of classic fashion design with interior design to set a mood.

> The principle of all the suites was to do something classic, yet with a modern line to it . . . like a Chanel suit. The tower suites are very much intended to be what I call the exhale in the Encore experience. The casino environments, the restaurants and the entertainment areas are all highly charged and dynamic. The suites were intended to provide a decompression.[9]

As a result of these shifts, clients now expect an emotional experience from entertainment facilities and the presentation of one. Nonetheless, many different approaches are utilized in the *Entice* segment, for instance, the association between the client's project goals and your design specialization. The Morgans Hotel Group selects designers who will reflect its legacy. Did you sell the client on selecting you for the project because of your unique talent or skill, and was this an important project goal for them? If so, it is imperative that this high priority goal be part of the opening statement and carry through the presented solutions. This does not need to be a very lengthy dialogue. When it is better said in the core segment, leave it out of the opening statement. Industry-specific jargon is best saved for the *Equate* segment of the presentation. You may utilize it in the event of a difficult sell. However, if you sold the client on LEED characteristics, state them in the concept opening. Also, highlight how the project met the LEED requirements in the closing segment. This is true for any high-priority project goal.

You might try some of the same techniques used by the writers of articles in design trade periodicals. Cassie Walker wrote this for *Interior Design* magazine:

> Facing the Gulf of Mexico in sunny, surf-friendly St. Petersburg, Florida, the bohemian Postcard Inn on the Beach is a place to write home about. . . . Now, that sounds like more than just a crash pad for spring break.[10]

▶ "When addressing the specific project goals, it's a good idea to begin with the most important drivers, and drill down in order of importance. An example: If creating a collaborative environment is an important project driver, then start with the elements of the design that contribute to the collaborative nature of the space." Alan Dandron, design principal at Mancini Duffy

Imagine a similar opening statement to create a preview of the project experience to engage your audience. By reading the complete article and viewing the project images, you can take cues to develop your own design project narration and fashion the individual design experience for the client.

Program Requirements

Alternately, your opening may simply focus on the program requirements. Accomplish this by detailing the facility needs, financial concerns, and social responsibilities. AAI clearly states this in its work for Hitachi in the last two sentences:

> The primary design challenge for Hitachi Global Storage Technologies' 366,000-square-foot international headquarters was to create an environment that facilitated collaboration and encouraged a sense of community between the corporate and research and development groups housed in this facility. Working within a limited budget, AAI transformed the massive, multi-story atrium at the core of the company's headquarters into a warm and inviting space. In addition, AAI designed open and private offices, training rooms, conference rooms, executive offices, and an executive boardroom. Color palettes, lighting improvements, furniture specifications, and custom signage were developed for the entire facility.[11]

When presenting, you may conclude any introduction by saying, "Today we will show you how we have accomplished these goals." Make the viewer curious enough before revealing the content in the core of the presentation.

Engage

The *Engage* segment is the core of the presentation and must deal with the client's program requests and demonstrate how you have solved all of the design issues. Additionally, it supports your central design concept and represents the client and its brand or image. You learned the language to apply to this segment in Chapter 1.

Here you unveil the solution with design-language savviness and visuals. Take this opportunity to direct the viewers to the characteristics you want them to notice. Identify, describe, and reveal the specific strengths and unique features of the design solution. Plan the visuals and transitions so they link the successive elements of the presentation, and be sure to make their relationship clear to the audience. Whatever you include, its primary purpose is to clarify, demonstrate, and provide visual examples to win the support of the client for the solution. That is, to get approval to continue to the next phase of the design process—the construction document phase. Remember that a designer is legally bound by a contract to execute these obligations.

To understand how this would work, let's consider an office project such as Artis Capital Management, designed by Rottet Studio, and use an example of a model presentation. Imagine yourself presenting the project solution to the client. A white box is sitting on the conference table between you and the client. *Entice* with an opening statement:

> The design team aimed to create a relaxing work space tailored to the company's unique culture, the San Francisco environment, and an environment that was more home than office to the 14-person trading team. The office is conceived as a *white box*. As the white planes peel away (your cue), the materials, textures, and colors behind are revealed, resulting in a *visually quiet* space that coun-

teracts the constant visual stimulation of multiple computer screens. No walls touch the perimeter and service areas are located around the core, allowing clear views throughout the space of the entire city.[12] (Figure 2.7)

At the cue, open the box while finishing the opening statement. Gently remove the top, place it nearby, inside up—it is the ceiling plan. Gently open the sides, letting them fold down—they are the color and material samples. The bottom of the box is the rendered floor plan—on top of it is a clear plastic box representing the perimeter window walls. Pause for a few moments to let the client absorb the experience and prepare them to focus their attention to your next statement.

Figure 2.7
Rottet Studio describes a "visually quiet" interior workspace concept for Artis Capital Management in San Francisco.

Describe the floor covering while pointing to the plan and the samples. Figure 2.8 illustrates the floor covering and concept behind the design and material choices.

Move the ceiling plan closer to the client. Describe the ceiling and the samples. Say, "Along the bay side, incisions are cut into the white box in the ceiling in a pattern that emulates barges in the bay. These incisions are carved away to reveal a warm wood material beyond and provide ambient light. The city side is more rigid and orthogonal, mimicking the city's grid pattern."[13]

Remove the plastic box and begin describing the plan. Say, "The six small offices double as mini art galleries. A giant door conceals the work area, and, when closed, the room is void of visual elements allowing the impressive art collection to be the feature. The lounge-style chairs with matching ottomans allow employees to retreat into their *home* and relax."[14]

The design as described above is the sum of a total experience for the end users. Forward-thinking aesthetics were engaged to represent the brand and culture of the client's company. The design of space supports their work needs and identity. Therefore, in this case, it is important to emphasize those facts in the closing statement.

The use of the white box for the presentation is not the only method to present this design in 3-D. Figures 2.9 and 2.10 show

Figure 2.8
If you were presenting this design you could say, "Custom carpet emulates water lapping on the shore. A dark gray cleft stone surrounds the entire floor between columns to reinforce the notion of rippling tides at the water's edge." *(Contemporist Blog; "Artis Capital Management Office Interior by Rottet Studio," blog entry by Dave, April 15, 2010, www.contemporist.com/2010/04/15/artis-capital-management-office-interior-by-rottet-studio/)*

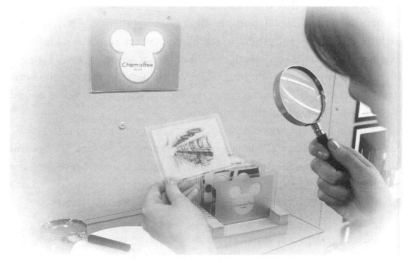

Figure 2.9
Chemistree by Kristyn Hill. *(Design © Kristyn Hill)*

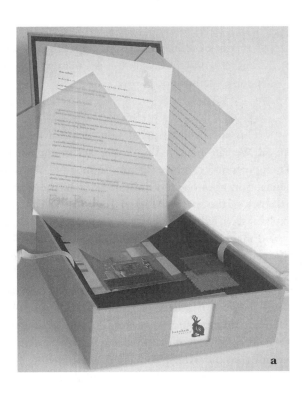

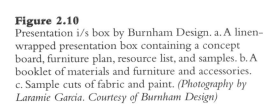

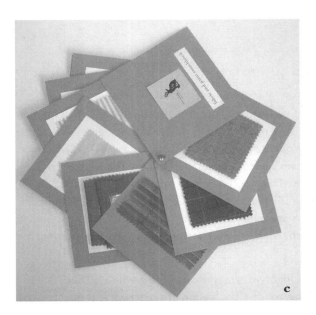

Figure 2.10
Presentation i/s box by Burnham Design. a. A linen-wrapped presentation box containing a concept board, furniture plan, resource list, and samples. b. A booklet of materials and furniture and accessories. c. Sample cuts of fabric and paint. *(Photography by Laramie Garcia. Courtesy of Burnham Design)*

imaginative presentation techniques. Professionals and students alike imagine unique solutions to deliver ideas. Vicente Wolf believes that:

> Good salesmanship will supersede any "newfangled" technology or tricks. I always present in the same way (a presentation is showbiz; it always has to have excitement and discovery) . . . renderings, plans, materials, and an estimate of fees. In presenting, our setup is to always have the samples/fabrics on a tray and covered up in the order of presentation. At the start of the presentations, I present walls, floors, window treatment, colors, upholstery, textiles/fabrics, case goods, furnishings, and lighting. A plan is cut up by room, so the client will focus room-by-room, and not be distracted. As I present, I fit all the pieces together to see the complete project put together.[15]

Energize

The conclusion of your presentation ought to have a convincing take-away message. At this point, you recap how the highlighted features fulfill the client's needs, project guidelines, and the overall concept. Summarize the main concepts, and reassert how the solution relates to issues you have raised. You could begin your closing by saying, "In summary . . . ," and avoid an awkward pause. A more polished approach is to prepare several statements that extract the essence of the design and thus imply a finish. Make these statements sincere and mesmerizing. For example:

> A place to which we can come and for a while be free from thinking about what we are going to do. It is not

a matter of scale, proportions, light efficiency, floor finishes, and white walls—it is a matter of awakening people's sensitivity.[16]

—Claudio Silvestrin

This approach to persuasion blends a logical and an emotional appeal. We can imagine this closing statement would inspire the client. The perception can be a deep metaphor of balance or connection. The description goes beyond the functions of the space by relating an experience of the space. Designer Tony Chi calls it "invisible design" and explains it as "what touches you rather than what you see."[17]

Finally, the closing is primarily a way to establish unity and conclusiveness for the presentation. An energizing closing statement may utilize many of the same ideas as the opening. You may recap the opening or the exact same remarks you used to entice the viewer, but with a new edge. It is a literary technique called bookending, where you reference the opening statement or quote or anecdote to add continuity. Returning to your most dynamic visual with the strongest representation of the overall concept is a compelling tool to use with your closing. Combine it with a compelling statement regarding what is at stake or what it has to do with the client by making it personal and limited to his or her present situation. What major problems did your design solve? Drive your main concept home and make your intentions clear in the closing.

Each important point you described in your presentation leads to the closing in some way, and you could close by firmly supporting your recommendations. It is important for clients to realize that you want them to approve the presentation, and your responsibility is to refocus their attention to that end. You could state very clearly, "With your approval, we are ready to begin the next phase of the project." Make the last sentence positive and do not fade out. Enjoy your first *exhale moment*, thank everyone, and ask for questions.

Equate

Equate is the collaboration opportunity in your presentation. This segment is when you take questions and obtain the client's consent to proceed. It is advisable to prepare for this stage by anticipating problems or questions the client may have and addressing them in your talk, before the audience has a chance to worry about them. Always leave time for questions and discussion; if you do not, key persons may need to leave the meeting before you obtain their approval to proceed.

Malcolm Gladwell, in his book *Blink: The Power of Thinking Without Thinking*, discusses the complexity of the thought process, which is often emotional rather than logical and linear. Based on Gladwell's investigation, many businesses are reconsidering the logical approach they traditionally take in appealing to their clients. He proves this point with the success of the Aeron chair by Herman Miller. The company trusted its instincts, which were contrary to testing data that showed very low aesthetic scores and poor receptions from focus groups. Gladwell emphasizes that the "most successful organizations of any kind—are the ones that understand how to combine rational analysis with instinctive judgment."[18]

Keeping this in mind, designers work to understand the blocks and fears that may prevent the client from accepting recommendations, and they build their presentations, to some extent, around alleviating those fears. You can help your clients connect to the solution in the way you address their questions and objections. Think of the decision process as an organic concert in which you and the client collectively produce the music. Remember that you are equals and co-creators in the process, regardless of your role as a professional. Your client may be an amateur or a pro at design. It is usual to find the client has built more projects than you have. Demonstrate your ability to work collaboratively, but use your skills to be persuasive. Effective strategies for collaboration are discussed in Chapter 7.

Designer Samuel Botero points out that the best results come from an open dialogue between designer and client. "Some clients resist solutions that may seem unfamiliar to them," Botero remarks.[19] "Others leave it all to the designer and do not participate in the process. A really successful interior develops from the synergy between client and designer." Here, too, humor is indispensable: "It helps lead a client to a new point of view, to relax the tension that can sometimes develop when people make unaccustomed decisions. For example, 'If *I* had to be a chair, *I'd be that one*' says reams more than, 'Oh, what a fabulous chair.' "[20] A skillfully coordinated group experience, such as this phase of a design presentation, is pleasurable. Enjoy your second exhale moment and thank everyone. Now, call the office and tell everyone about the success!

The presentation is a libretto, and here you have the design opera layers to follow for your presentation. *Entice* is the overture and *Engage* may include an aria, chorus, duet, trio, and recitative—or two or three. Intermission please! *Energize* is the finale, and do return for your curtain call in the *Equate* segment.

Dialogue with John R. Sadlon

Mancini Duffy, New York, New York
John R. Sadlon, Managing Principal

Q. Is there a company style of presenting, or does each presentation evolve out of the nature of the project? What is your approach? Do you use the same approach for all of your presentations?

A. In preparation, key factors include confirming the client/audience's primary "hot buttons" or main business drivers, precisely determining the "message" to be delivered, crafting the words, and preparing the design visuals necessary to convey your concept effectively, and dedicating sufficient time to rehearse the various components of your presentation.

With regard to delivery, your approach should focus on sequencing the various components of your message. This should begin with a concise statement of the primary goals and objectives of the project, as well as a mission statement of your unique design approach, and go on to elaborate on the specific details of your design solution.... At the close of your presentation, succinctly restate your unique design approach, and give the client/audience a compelling reason to select your proposed solution.[21]

Idea Exchange

- A brief interview with Kazuyo Sejima of SANNA can be viewed at *Architectural Digest* online: www.architecturaldigest.com/video?videoID=17523712001.
- Macquarie Group Limited, One Shelly Street, Sydney, Australia. One Shelley Street is an effort to reframe the requirements and performance of the twenty-first-century office. Clive Wilkinson Architects implemented a radical, large-scale workplace design that leverages mobility, transparency, multiple tailor-made work settings, destination work plazas, follow-me technology, and carbon neutral systems. Go to the link and view Wilkinson on video as he describes the project: www.clivewilkinson.com/feature/macquarie_video.html.

Create Experience

Probe

Part one. Read the editorials and articles about a feature design project. Study the style of the sentences used to describe the space. Extract the dialogue that would be important to include in a design presentation.

Part two. Study the exterior of Neiman Marcus, Natick, Massachusetts in Figure 2.4. Prepare an opening statement for the design to entice the viewer. Repeat the same for one of your design projects.

Engage

Part one. Research the project Maison Moschino, Milan, Italy. Write a concept statement for the hotel project.

Part two. Develop a design presentation narrative for the public spaces and three room designs.

Alternate: Use your own project and do the same.

3 Viewer Experience

*A*nd so, in the end, can a spirit be said to have come forward in this new building, and if so, what kind? *"The thing no one tells you about Axel [Vervoordt]'s work until you live with it,"* Trudy Cejas observes, *"is how serene it is. Whenever I walk into this house, my shoulders drop. It's the strangest thing."*

"Not so very strange," says Vervoordt. *"Interior design is a kind of magic. Never underestimate the power of the human hand. What I'd hoped for here was the flavor of a big Italian house with little corners balanced and worked to look like jewels."*[1]

— Michael Frank, *Architectural Digest*

The experience of a space has personal meaning for individuals and can trigger positive emotions. A home is the core of emotional identity, and for the past 10 years, design psychologists have been advocating environmental self-reflection to uncover a client's vision of ideal place.[2] This process involves exploring past, present, and future links between self and place. The purpose is to go beyond the practical aspects of space into deeper psychic wholeness—a personal design autobiography. Not only does this portrait of a client translate into individual design solutions for him or her, but it can also lead to a positive experience for the design presentations. Each person has a unique point of view regarding what makes a space a positive experience.

Perception

Designers watch what people do and what they do not do. Likewise, we listen to what they say and what they do not say. Even small details give us great clues about behavior, unmet needs, or the reasons why someone may like blue. Don't forget what you learned about your audience when preparing the design brief—instead put it to use again for the presentation. Properly focusing attention on human emotions and perceptions as well as their influence on design is a huge challenge (Figure 3.1).

Moreover, the characteristics of our clients directly influence our methods of presenting, including the details and the words. A focused presentation is always mindful of those characteristics. Our stakeholders, or end users, are from multiple generations, who have been described as including Traditionalist (born before 1946) or the silent generation (1928–1945), baby boomers (1946–1953), generation Jones (1954–1965), generation X (1965–1979), generation Y or millennials (1980–2000), and the future adult generations, I and Alpha (A). Popular culture shaped generational names and these names are derivatives of

historical events, social or demographic change, or a big change in the calendar. While there are different attitudes, lifestyles, and values among generations, keep in mind that the same is true within generations.

The presentation strategy must also take into consideration that language influences emotions and reactions. Clients are not buying interior design—they are buying a solution that satisfies deeper needs. That requires empathy on your part and the ability to step into their shoes and gain insight into their behaviors. The design is their story and how your ideas satisfy their needs. Find the values there. Tap into the possible motivation under the surface that drives clients' decisions. We need to know more than whether they like a traditional sofa versus a modern sofa design or gray versus yellow. We can also study the common and unique values of cultural generations.

▶ "Good communicators are empiricists at heart—they know that what they say doesn't really matter, it's what the audience hears that really counts. They don't judge their success by what they were 'trying' to say . . . they judge their success by whether or not the audience 'gets it.' "
Scott Simpson, principal and senior director at Kling Stubbins

Emotions

Emotions have a strong effect on clients' experiences of a presentation; therefore, you must be attuned to those emotions in order to influence them with interventions. Designers formulate a presentation with a careful balance of logic and intuition—just as they solve the design problem. For example, you can persuade by using the concepts of *what* and *why*. *What* represents the client signing off on the design; *why* represents the reasoning you present. *Why* is directed to logical proof or an emotional appeal. If you are using proof, the *why* is focused on the design subjects. When you are appealing to emotions, the *why* is

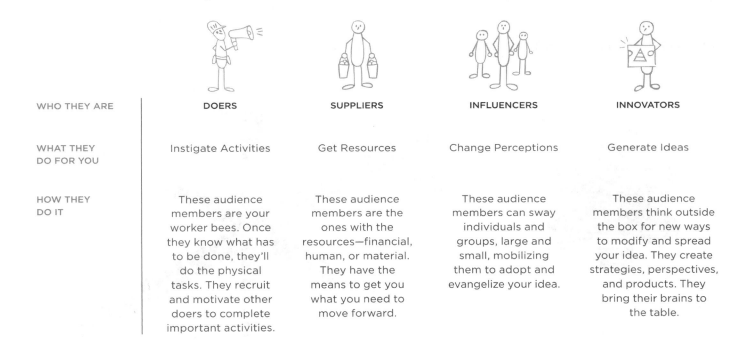

	DOERS	**SUPPLIERS**	**INFLUENCERS**	**INNOVATORS**
WHO THEY ARE				
WHAT THEY DO FOR YOU	Instigate Activities	Get Resources	Change Perceptions	Generate Ideas
HOW THEY DO IT	These audience members are your worker bees. Once they know what has to be done, they'll do the physical tasks. They recruit and motivate other doers to complete important activities.	These audience members are the ones with the resources—financial, human, or material. They have the means to get you what you need to move forward.	These audience members can sway individuals and groups, large and small, mobilizing them to adopt and evangelize your idea.	These audience members think outside the box for new ways to modify and spread your idea. They create strategies, perspectives, and products. They bring their brains to the table.

Figure 3.1

The audience as defined by Nancy Duarte, Duarte Design, Mountain View, CA: The first meeting with your client is where you begin your observations and plan for the specific information, gathering steps to follow. Your observations are just as important for the presentation and design solution as is your applied knowledge of psychology, social studies, and anthropology. *(Duarte, Nancy,* Resonate: Present Visual Stories that Transform Audiences *[Indianapolis: Wiley, 2010], 43)*

focused on the reactions of the viewers in the presentation. They both are powerful motivators if blended well to support your design concepts. When you know the client or audience well, you can develop a genuine tone of emotional appeal (Figures 3.2 and 3.3). One example of a group focused on finding that balance is The Design & Emotion Society, which "raises issues and facilitates dialogue among practitioners, researchers, and industry, in order to integrate salient themes of emotional experience into the design profession."[3] The Design & Emotion

MODELS OF CUSTOMER EXPERIENCE

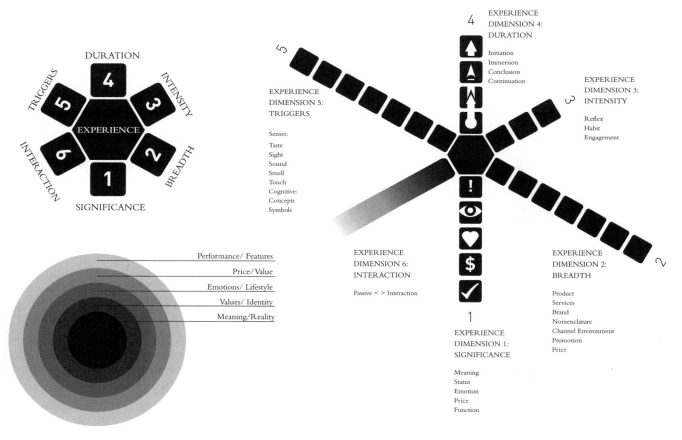

Figure 3.2
Models of Customer Experience as defined by Nathan Shedroff: In using proof the *why* is focused on the design subjects. When you are appealing to emotions the *why* is focused on the reactions of the viewers in the presentation. *(Shedroff, Nathan, "Models of Customer Experience,"* Interactions *[November–December 2008], 40)*

SIX DIMENSIONS OF EXPERIENCE

Breath (consistency across touchpoints)

Intensity

Duration (time)

Triggers (how sensorial and cognitive choices are interpreted by customers)

Interaction

Significance (diagram)

FIVE LEVELS OF SIGNIFICANCE

Meaning (Reality)	How does this fit into my world?
Status/Identity (Values)	Is this me?
Emotions (Lifestyle)	How does this make me feel?
Price (Value)	Does this meet my expectations of value?
Function (Performance)	Does this do what I need done?

15 CORE MEANINGS

Accomplishment	Justice
Beauty	Oneness
Creation	Redemption
Community	Security
Duty	Truth
Enlightenment	Validation
Freedom	Wonder
Harmony	

Figure 3.3
Experience, Significance, and Meanings of Customer Experience as defined by
Nathan Shedroff. *(Shedroff, Nathan, "Models of Customer Experience,"* Interactions
[November–December 2008], 41)

Society is an international network of researchers, designers, and industry that aims at stimulating emotion and experience-driven design. Although the initiative originated from the discipline of product design and design research, through the years practitioners from other design disciplines, such as interaction design and branding design, have contributed and benefited from the network and activities. Bring into play the studies and point of view of experience-driven design, because it is equally applicable to interior design and makes it more interesting.

> ▶ "So much of what I do is about how people live, and I am always looking for balance. I love it when rooms come alive with a personality, and I like things to be real and honest and reflect the people who live there. We designers definitely have a point of view, but it depends where a home is and who the people are and what they like. It's a process. You ask lots of questions and you listen. It's the listening and the seeing and the feeling—it's all about the senses." Victoria Hagan, interior designer

Cultures

Keep in mind that not only are you designing for and working with multiple adult generations, including traditionalist (18 percent), baby boomers (15 percent), generation Jones (26 percent), generation X (21 percent), and generation Y (20 percent), business organizational types are also changing to create a workplace to satisfy the needs of the employees. Historically, most business functions, from accounting to operations and even marketing, are focused on optimization and standardization.[4] This is the Control (hierarchy) Culture. Additional ways that companies work and represent themselves are Compete (market) Culture, Collaborate (clan) Culture, and Create (adhocracy) Culture (Figure 3.4). The MBA programs of many schools are now educating business students

"Collaborate (Clan)" Culture

An open and friendly place to work where people share a lot of themselves. It is like an extended family. Leaders are considered to be mentors or even parental figures. Group loyalty and sense of tradition are strong. There is an emphasis on the long-term benefits of human resources development and great importance is given to group cohesion. There is a strong concern for people. The organization places a premium on teamwork, participation, and consensus.

"Create (Adhocracy)" Culture

A dynamic, entrepreneurial, and creative place to work. Innovation and risk-taking are embraced by employees and leaders. A commitment to experimentation and thinking differently are what unify the organization. They strive to be on the leading edge. The long-term emphasis is on growth and acquiring new resources. Success means gaining unique and new products or services. Being an industry leader is important. Individual initiative and freedom are encouraged.

"Control (Hierarchy)" Culture

A highly structured and formal place to work. Rules and procedures govern behavior. Leaders strive to be good coordinators and organizers who are efficiency-minded. Maintaining a smooth-running organization is most critical. Formal policies are what hold the group together. Stability, performance, and efficient operations are the long-term goals. Success means dependable delivery, smooth scheduling, and low cost. Management wants security and predictablity.

"Compete (Market)" Culture

A results-driven organization focused on job completion. People are competitive and goal-oriented. Leaders are demanding, hard-driving, and productive. The emphasis on winning unifies the organization. Reputation and success are common concerns. Long-term focus is on competitive action and achievement of measurable goals and targets. Sucess means market share and penetration. Competitive pricing and market leadership are important.

Figure 3.4
The four organizational culture types are easy to understand; however, designers still must consider deeper subdominant traits. *(Tharp, Bruce M., "Four Organizational Culture Types,"* Haworth: Organizational Culture White Paper *[April 2009], 5. www.haworth.com/en-us/Knowledge/Workplace-Library/Documents/Four-Organizational-Culture-Types_6.pdf)*

to be innovative by using the creative design process. The new Create corporate executive leaders are using design thinking in many parts of their organizations to inspire and transform services, products, and solutions. Look for ways to understand the client's business culture in order to help you design for them and understand how they make decisions.

This will give you greater appreciation for all business functions and issues. Says Bill Bouchey, design director at M Moser:

> We have found that European and American companies in Asia are generally more progressive and emphasize environments that reflect activity-based work more literally. They have higher utilization rates and less hierarchy, achieving higher employee satisfaction. In North America, this finding is less common across the board.[5]

Analysis

Now, let's get back to our practical inquiries regarding attendees. The very first fact you need to know before fully developing the final presentation is who the viewers are. You will be able to read the room beforehand once you determine who will be in the room. This applies to practitioners and students as well as to clients. The audiences for a design presentation are actually willing participants and have been contributing to the project throughout its duration. It is easier to work with them because they want to be there and you have an established relationship. They are not expecting a long and highly detailed explanation of the project. This audience is more interested in the interpretation and analysis of your ideas with focused material.

Viewers
Presently, a service economy prevails; therefore, you must deliberately design an engaging experience for the viewer. They are expecting a memorable and personal experience. They are the guests and you are the stager. Base your script for the presentation on exploring who they are. Prepare an attendee inquiry as shown in Figure 3.5 and tailor the presentation accordingly.

Figure 3.5
Attendee inquiry.

How many are attending?
- On client side
- From design office
- Outside participants

Who are they?
- Name and title
- What is their expertise?
- What are their responsibilites?
- What is their design or technical background?
- What do they know about the project?

WHO

What are their needs?
- What will interest them?
- What do they care about most?
- What is least important to them?
- How will you organize the presentation in the best way for them?
- What do you want them to think, assume, or learn about you?
- Are you doing anything in the presentation that may surprise them?

WHAT

Why are they attending?
- To approve
- To be informed
- To assist and inform
- To observe
- Will they know the purpose of the presentation?
- What do they need to know from the presentation?
- What do they need to do with the information they acquire from you?
- How do or did they influence the design problem or the presentation? Did they review the design at different stages?

WHY

What are the special considerations?
- Subject matter knowledge
- Language
- Cultural
- Physical limitations
- Other issues such as dietary needs

NOTES

◄ **39** ►

VIEWER EXPERIENCE

Knowing as much as you can about client expectations and experience in the design industry will help you to clearly communicate with your viewers. Most persons attending a final design presentation will know the purpose, the project, and your firm. You need to build support early and keep them informed about the project benefits. When you can anticipate where any objections may be coming from, you can win their support by planning solutions to address objections before the presentation. Their authority or influence, and concern or interest, for the project is one method to classify them. The client does not view the classification exercise. It is a model that works for prioritizing interior design clients. Organize participants into four groups, as Figure 3.6 shows, and emphasize that level of interest matters more than level of influence or power because interest reflects enough care to defend or oppose project ideas. Call upon this group to support your concepts and recommendations during meetings and presentations when needed. However, during a presentation focus your attention on the most important person in attendance—the one who is giving the final approval. It is an honor and major responsibility to present to shareholders. When delivering to this audience type or members of a board, professionalism is vital. When they are involved, address the highest-level executive and make sure that the executive of the company signs off in the end. Those same VIPs may not attend a presentation but still have a stake and decision-making capacity.

Accordingly, your role is to make everyone your campaigner. Sometimes it may be a relative, informed about design, who will give clues and seek confirmation that the client is in safe hands. For instance, if choosing a textile of the same quality from different manufacturers, include a Donghia textile when you know that a close relative of your residential client loves Donghia textiles and has great influence over your client. Sometimes it takes only a simple gesture to win them over. Don't forget to consider the diversity of your viewers and arrange for a foreign language translator if needed.

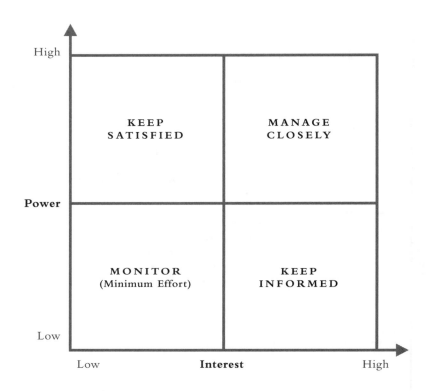

Figure 3.6
Influence/Interest categories as developed by Mind Tools. The file can be downloaded at www.mindtools.com/pages/article/newPPM_07.htm.

When you make the call to the client to clarify the details of the attendees, ask about any newcomers. When newcomers who were not in attendance at the previous development phase meetings plan to attend a current meeting, you will want to know more about them. Their presence can lead to presentation difficulties in the form of misunderstandings and loss of progress. For that reason, you may have to ask the client whether you should summarize what has been approved to date for the new viewers or whether the client will do it preceding the upcoming presentation. This is an excellent time to ask the client to review the project goals with staff, confirm previous approvals, and clarify what to expect in the next presentation.

Another consideration may be whether you want to request that specific individuals be present at the meeting. There are times when you need other design industry professionals to attend. They could include your consultants or those hired by the client. Their function might be to explain details or answer questions about specific project details beyond your expertise. These professionals may include lighting designers, audio visual specialists, marketing experts, graphic designers, architects or engineers, general contractors or builders, and real estate professionals. The main purpose is for them to present their portion of a project or answer client questions that you direct to them. They are your allies. You also have allies on the client team, and you may need to call on them to support a decision. The business client of today assembles teams that include a wide range of disciplines, resulting in an overlap in responsibilities and activities. This new interdisciplinary environment commonly includes chief executive officers, chief financial officers, chief technical officers, journalists, filmmakers, engineers, marketing and business experts, psychologists, scientists, and designers with MBAs or psychology degrees. A word of caution: too many people in attendance can lead to a presentation going off course and down the wrong path.

> It helps to simplify your message content and limit the number of important points you focus on in a given presentation. When in doubt, ask your client for guidance.

> "Try to keep the meeting as small as possible. With a residential client, *only* [italics added] the client will be in the meeting. I will not allow an audience, as they usually have a comment that I do not want to hear. [Whoever] worked on the project with me attends and takes notes during the presentation." Vicente Wolf, Vicente Wolf Associates, New York

Invisible Audience

You may have an invisible audience, not attending the presentation, including friends, family, colleagues, or other acquaintances of your client whose opinions and advice the client values, in addition to the viewers of your presentation. The invisible audience may create a few tricky surprises after the presentation. Although rarely, occasionally you might leave presentation materials with your client for review by the unseen VIP. A few days later, you may receive a call from your primary contact asking you to change something. Be aware that the contact may tell you exactly how to change it. Try to find a middle ground by working cooperatively with your client.

One the other hand, the hidden neighbor, relative, or colleague of the client may be worse. Occasionally, these people have influence on a residential or small commercial client. Their personal preferences may dominate the opinions offered. Diplomatically guide your client by reassuring them why your design recommendations are the right choice and why the solution is right for the client—not the well-meaning neighbor.

Students and practitioners may also have a hidden audience when submitting a project for a design competition or closed review process. They could include clients, design professionals, subject matter experts, instructors and professors, educational program directors, deans, manufacturers' representatives, book and periodical editors, board members of professional organizations, sponsors, and governmental agency representatives, to name a few. In this case, the presentation graphics must be very clear to tell the design story in a coherent and logical way. Also, clarify how you solved the requirements of the project brief or design program.

Jargon

A humorous characterization of the jargon of the design industry from ArtLex: Art Dictionary, an online dictionary, reminds us of how peculiar we sound: "The jargon of architecture is what architects and designers archly call 'talkitecture.'" Does the client audience know the jargon of the industry or the concepts you are presenting, or are these new to him or her? You may have to target your language so that it is appropriate. This does not mean that you speak down or up to the attendees. If you do, you may insult them. Don't use unfamiliar terms unless you can provide clear explanations. Find out from your client contact what he or she already knows about the project, design theory, and the design process. Keep in mind that most clients will have less design and technical experience than you.

Design Expressions

Also remember all industries streamline communication with jargon or shoptalk a great deal. You are an interior design specialist with a vocabulary of precise terminology. What are your specialist phrases, acronyms, and words? Be considerate when using jargon. Will your audience understand what it means? Do you need it to support your solution? During a presentation, it is more important to use terminology that your audience can comprehend rather than demonstrating

your knowledge of professional interior design vocabulary. With any audience, carefully translate the acronym or terms into plain English; otherwise, they may not understand your point or may be intimidated. In order to use jargon, you must explain the terms and substantiate the premise throughout the presentation. Keep definitions short by classifying the terms in a category of similar ideas or objects; then describe their special characteristics.

Client Expressions

Likewise, all businesses also have their own specialist jargon. Make sure you understand the jargon of the client's industry. Misinterpretations of words occur because of completely different meanings in other industries. Limit the amount of technical jargon and be aware of those who know as much or more, as they could challenge your concepts. In that case, watch out for hidden agendas, large egos, or professional jealousies.

Student Reviews

Juries, reviews, and critiques are unique audience groups for studio course work. They include teachers; tutors; fellow students; and visiting critics such as interior designers, specialists, related professionals, and even clients and users. When the presentation is graded, the instructor or the jury members are the most important people in the room. Although an instructor may be the only reviewer, it is important for students to show that they understand, know, and have solved all of the project needs. Assume that your instructor is an intelligent but uninformed observer.

Design Portfolios, by Diane M. Bender, covers the topic of student portfolio audiences in detail. A portfolio review audience varies depending on whether your objective is to continue your education or to find employment. Bender explains how to tailor a portfolio and frame a meeting to an audience group. Chances are, there will be more than one interviewer and more than one interview. The viewers can include principals, design directors, human resources directors, or sales or marketing managers for a design employment interview. Academic audiences may be juries, deans, program directors, professors, advisory boards, scholarship sponsors, or design professionals. Use the audience questions outlined in Figure 3.5 to help you define the viewers and tailor the meetings accordingly. Consequently, once you know who will be present, you can refine the plans for the venue.

Dialogue with John R. Sadlon

Mancini Duffy, New York, N.Y.
John R. Sadlon, Managing Principal

Q. If you were presenting to a board of directors, what would your approach be?

A. One fundamental element of any presentation is knowing your audience as well as anticipating their primary areas of concern. If [you're] presenting to a board of directors, it's likely that they will have a specific set of criteria upon which they will evaluate your presentation. In addition to a design solution that addresses the initial needs of the end user, a board of directors is more likely to focus on the long-term viability of your design. They may ask various questions: How flexible is your design solution to accommodate future changes in end-user needs? How responsive is your design solution to the ongoing maintenance and repair costs over the life cycle of the space? What initial costs are estimated for the work, and what long-term savings could be achieved by implementing alternative solutions?

Frequently, members of a board are not experienced in reading floor plans or details that are commonly understood within the design industry. In this case, your presentation may also need to include supplemental visuals such as axonometric drawings, rendered perspective drawings, and/or models to convey your design solution effectively.

It's likely that a board of directors is accountable for making long-term decisions that impact numerous groups or constituencies within an organization. Typically, it's unrealistic to believe that every need of each unique group can be accommodated within a comprehensive design solution. In these cases, the board is likely to approve solutions that effectively address the primary general needs of the entire organization rather than the unique needs of each individual subgroup.

It is also important to understand the decision-making process of the board. Does each member have an equal vote in the approval process, or is there ultimately one individual who makes the final decision? If decision is by consensus, it will be important for your design solution to take into account the various priorities of each board member. If decision is by one individual, your design solution may be slightly different to ensure compliance with that person's key objectives.

Idea Exchange

- Watch the video, "Wired to Care," wherein Heather Fraser from Rotman Designworks interviews Dev Patnaik of Jump Associates: www.youtube.com/watch?v=RVnx2vAlCvE&feature=player_embedded.

Create Experience

Fast Familiarity

The intent is to build up conversational skills for professional social contact. This exercise is performed by a group of people who are just beginning to work together. To prepare, set chairs in a circle.

- Each person thinks of two questions to ask a new acquaintance and writes them down on a blank sheet of paper. For example: What is your favorite film? What is the most interesting thing you have done in the last week? What is the funniest thing that ever happened to you?
- When done writing, group members move quickly around the circle asking each other the questions and noting each answer, including the responder's name, on the paper. Stop this activity when most of the group members have interacted.
- Ask individuals to stand up one by one and state their names. Have the others in the group shout out some of the things about this person that they just learned.

Personality Profiles

The purpose of the exercise is to substantiate decisions for the diverse users in a project. Link to the Design Council site and complete the exercise: www.designcouncil.org.uk/about-design/How-designers-work/Design-methods/Character-Profiles/.

Stakeholder Communication

The intent of this exercise is to plan how to manage communication with diverse users. Link to the Mind Tools site and complete a Stakeholder Planning exercise. www.mindtools.com/pages/article/newPPM_08.htm.

4 Intention and Context of Presentation

Then one day the White House called. They were beginning work on the president's library and wanted advice. Clinton and I had a lot of "good old boy" stories. . . . When I got the call from the White House inviting me to lunch, I asked who else would be there and was told, "Just the president's lawyers." So I replied, "Should I bring mine?"[1]

— Bill Lacy, architect

Think about the type of presentation you plan to give. Is it an informal discussion or a formal presentation with protocol requirements? Each has its own purpose. Bill Lacy clarified the details of attendees with a witty reply and knew the objective of his meeting in advance. Lacy, an experienced architectural consultant, also acts as a juror for various reviews and advises clients on choosing an architect for a particular project. Not all meetings are formal and not all presentations are for final design approval. The design process involves meetings and presentations at several stages, from preliminary to final. For instance, a successful schematic design presentation leads to the final design presentation; a winning final design presentation opens the door to the construction document and purchasing phase.

Intentions

Consider the intent of your presentation before you begin to organize your material. Usually an intention places the design in a larger context and gives both designers and clients reasons to be interested in the project. Clients like to know why you, the designer, care about their particular project and how you can meet their needs. Opinions vary among designers—interior designers, set designers, graphic designers, fashion designers, product designers, and architects—regarding the intention of their work. This is understandable because their work situations and backgrounds vary greatly.

The goals of your presentation may be to start a dialogue with the client; to educate; to improve a design; to describe design work; to motivate the client to buy; to introduce end users to different cultures and alternative viewpoints; to place the solution in a historical, cultural, environmental, or political context; and, finally, to entertain the client or end user. Harry Schnaper likes to educate his clients and watch them evolve because he feels that it is a large part of what designers do. He often includes period or important furniture in his interiors:

> They need to hear the spiel (story); they need to hear the background, who Jean Royère was, when he produced his furniture, who made it, what it is selling at [sic], what it's worth, why you should buy it, and why you should be proud of owning it.[2]

Presentations have strategic value to end users, designers, and clients, as summarized in Figure 4.1. Today, design is becoming increasingly complex and referential, constantly being brought to the fore by either implication or association. Therefore, you should be able to place the design solution in context for your client. Design expresses culture, identity, emotion, and environment. Designer Shashi Caan told the 2010 graduates of New York School of Interior Design this:

> While there are many experts looking at evolving and sustaining our physical world, the interior designer has the sole responsibility of also thinking about the qualities of our human existence within our surroundings. We are the professionals that must, to ensure emotional, perceptual, behavioral and sensory satisfaction at both a cultural and a global level.[3]

▶ "My focus, since my first project, was to integrate the arts. I think that architecture and fine art should come together. When I make a building, I'm not satisfied until I know that it inspires awe, that it inspires feeling." Oscar Niemeyer, architect

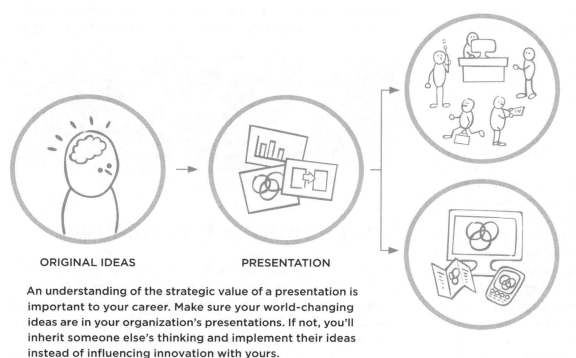

ACTIVITIES

After the ideas are presented and agreed to, work activities are generated from the presentations. Most presentations persuade people to take action, so presentations spawn a lot of activity.

MEDIA

Also, after the brilliant thinking in the presentation is solidified, it ripples through and informs other related materials needed to support and spread the idea like websites, social media, brochures, and so forth.

ORIGINAL IDEAS   PRESENTATION

An understanding of the strategic value of a presentation is important to your career. Make sure your world-changing ideas are in your organization's presentations. If not, you'll inherit someone else's thinking and implement their ideas instead of influencing innovation with yours.

Remember, just because you communicated your idea once doesn't mean you're done. It takes several presentations delivered over and over to make an idea become reality. Well-prepared presentations will speed up the adoption and change your world!

Figure 4.1
Strategic value of a presentation as envisioned by Nancy Duarte, Duarte Design. This is the challenge: Be intelligent about how you decide to communicate your solutions visually. *(Duarte, Nancy,* Resonate: Present Visual Stories that Transform Audiences *[Indianapolis: Wiley, 2010], 197)*

As one of those professionals, you should ask yourself a few important questions before you begin work on your presentation:

- What is this presentation about?
- What is its objective?
- What are the key aspects of this presentation?
- How should I engage the client?

Each type of presentation may call for different presenters, depending on which design project team members are most involved. Similarly, each presentation may address a varied group of individuals on the client side. You must know everything about the specific clients you are speaking to at each stage, as noted in Chapter 3.

Finally, you must consider context in relation to the physical environment for the presentation. The physical space, or venue, and audience are discussed in Chapter 6. Meetings with the design and consulting teams occur on many levels—in person, videoconferencing and links for impromptu videoconferencing, instant messaging, and discussion boards. Collaboration relies on dynamic interaction tools, and e-mail is not the most effective way to support this. Face-to-face meetings are the best way to interpret other nuances of communication, such as body language. Meetings between the client, designer, and other consultants are not new ways of collaborating. The sharing of graphic information and specifications between designers, owners, and consultants is Integrative Practice (IP). What is different now is the rapid pace of sharing the information throughout the design process among all of these collaborators. Building Information Modeling (BIM) is the software technology that allows the instant information sharing to happen.

Of equal importance, you must determine what type of design presentation you are planning in order to provide the appropriate materials for the presentation. The intent of a final design presentation is not the same as that of an informational presentation for the client's

employees. Likewise, a presentation for a civic design competition varies significantly from one meant to help a client secure funds for a project.

▶ "As designers and architects, we have the tremendous opportunity to tell stories . . . whether they are about a chef, a menu, a cuisine, a location, or a hotel chain. We have the gift each and every time we lift a pen or pencil to tell a story. That's why I do this!" Glen Coben, Glen & Company

Design Process Presentations

This chapter will not go into detail about the design process. Enough excellent books do just that. This chapter briefly defines the process in its respective phases and discusses the presentations associated with each stage. Before we can do that, a review of design contracts or agreements is necessary. The contract is the established guideline for a designer's commitment to a project. It clearly outlines the tasks that the designer will perform for the client. That also includes when, how, and why information will be presented. Action is required on the part of the designer and the client.

In general, professional designers follow the design process to create solutions for their clients but present solutions in sequential phases of a design, and these are specified by the contract or agreement with the client. Sample contracts available from ASID outline the scope of services for an interior design project. The phases (Figure 4.2), in addition to initiating presentations, also determine billing periods for the design office. Once a phase is approved, the client is billed for the services completed for that segment of the project.

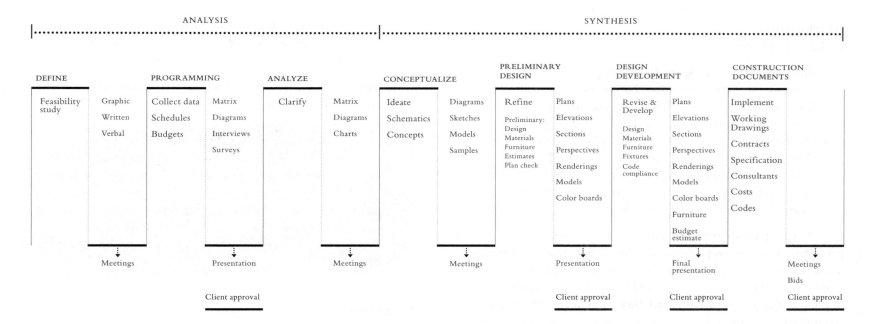

| ANALYSIS | | | | | SYNTHESIS | | | |

| DEFINE | | PROGRAMMING | | ANALYZE | | CONCEPTUALIZE | | PRELIMINARY DESIGN | | DESIGN DEVELOPMENT | | CONSTRUCTION DOCUMENTS |

Feasibility study — Graphic / Written / Verbal — Collect data / Schedules / Budgets — Matrix / Diagrams / Interviews / Surveys — Clarify — Matrix / Diagrams / Charts — Ideate / Schematics / Concepts — Diagrams / Sketches / Models / Samples — Refine — Preliminary: Design Materials Furniture Estimates Code Plan check — Plans / Elevations / Sections / Perspectives / Renderings / Models / Color boards — Revise & Develop — Design Materials Furniture Fixtures Code compliance — Plans / Elevations / Sections / Perspectives / Renderings / Models / Color boards / Furniture / Budget estimate — Implement / Working Drawings / Contracts / Specification / Consultants / Costs / Codes

Meetings — Presentation — Meetings — Meetings — Presentation — Final presentation — Meetings / Bids

Client approval — Client approval — Client approval — Client approval

Figure 4.2
Design Process and Presentations per stages. The phases initiate presentations. After completing one phase, the designer obtains a formal approval from the client before proceeding to the next phase. The approval process protects both the client and the designer. In essence, the previous presentations during the design process are the exposition for the final design presentation. That is, they give information needed to understand and move on to later design refinements.

In order for designers to be successful and profitable, they must manage the time constraints of the project and budget the staff time. Be prudent about your use of time to visually communicate your solutions. Students and designers often say they could do a better job if they had more time. That raises many eyebrows with design firm principals. As the late Al Cruz, AIA, MCG Architects, responded to his staff: "Even a gorilla can come up with a great design solution and presentation if given enough time."

▶ "You had to produce some credible drawings in order to bill the client. (Carlo) Scarpa would sometimes start a project by saying, 'I have to have a door like this,' even before deciding on the basic design of the building. Well, if you have a client who is expecting a house, you can't just show a sketch of a beautiful door and expect to get paid. Scarpa often did not bill until the end of the project, because it was not until then that he actually had something real to show." Marco Frascari

Marketing

Architect Bill Lacy states:

> Interviews are the make-or-break thing. You have to un-
> derstand what the client wants. Forget about everything
> but the client's project. Clients don't take the same keen
> interest in what you've done as in what you're going to
> do for them. I've seen architects fail by being arrogant.
> The top architects are generally excited about the pos-
> sibilities of what a project can be and how they can do
> it. It's that intensity about the client's project that's more
> important than almost anything else.[4]

Keeping Lacy's comments in mind, be aware that a marketing
presentation meeting is primarily a conversation and way of getting to
know the person first; then the proposed project details are discussed. In
doing this, you establish a rapport and learn how to communicate and
respond to this particular individual. Be a good listener. If this goes well,
the portfolio of work takes its proper place in the equation. Better yet,
the client will begin to offer the details of the project. It is an excellent
clue that she or he is seriously considering you for hire. Of course, there
is always the chance that the client wants on-the-spot recommendations to compare with those from other designers who have been inter-
viewed. Be careful in responding—leave yourself open to explore the
project when you are signed on.

By extension, tell a story about each project as you review your
portfolio work. Let the client set the pace as they flip through the pages.
Take your cue when they pause at an image. Christian Hogue of Architect Profits, Inc. suggests:

> Instead of explaining what one does as far as technical
> greatness, simply let prospects know what solutions you
> can provide to the problems and fears they have. People
> who are considering building or remodeling anything
> all have fears and problems and are looking for

solutions. Understanding this problem/solution format is
an important first step to understanding how to promote
in ways that generate prospects and business.[5]

Many designers describe the design process to the client only after
reviewing the project details.

> ▶ "Also give consideration to the fact that your client or audience may
> be interviewing other designers as part of a competitive process. Who
> will your competitors be? What relationships do your competitors have
> with the client/audience? Ask yourself how these relationships might
> influence the thoughts and opinions of your client/audience. Given
> these factors, strategize the ways in which you can make the most
> compelling presentation possible." John R. Sadlon, managing principal
> at Mancini Duffy

Programming

In the programming phase, designers will gather the details about the
project, research the related issues, and formulate a plan of action for
a project. A series of meetings are required to ask the client critical
questions, survey employees, or survey an existing architectural space.
The designer meets with all key stakeholders to understand the requirements and viewpoints. For instance, with commercial space, these sessions help the designer understand the office culture, what the client
wants the design to communicate to others, possible future business
changes, and flexibility of the work environment. This discovery and
orientation leads the design team to a definition of the project. The vision and design program that evolves from this information is presented
to the client, and it may require many meetings before the final approval
to proceed occurs. During these meetings, you build a relationship and
spirit of collaboration with the client in addition to solving the design
problem. Use this opportunity to be genuinely interested in their concerns, as it serves to gain client confidence early in the process. Your

continued professional manner in the information-gathering meetings leads to more successful presentations.

As a result, the size of the project determines the extent of the documents required for progress meetings during this phase. The progress meetings, in-house and with the client team, are often lengthy and fluid because a large amount of information goes through a progression of analysis and synthesis. A designer enlists the right blend of stakeholders with influence. They are not always those with seniority or title. Those in an organization who do the work instead of manage the work can offer great insight to what is actually happening in their workplace.

Once the goals are established and the components of the project clearly defined, the designer presents the design program or brief to the client. A well-constructed brief will allow for serendipity, unpredictability, and the capricious whims of fate, for that is the creative realm from which breakthrough ideas emerge.[6] Figures 4.3 through 4.6 show how the information gathered in the early design phases are organized for the presentation to define a project direction for the client. The documents for a formal presentation meeting during this phase could include:

- A written design concept or program statement
- A written program defining the project, including spatial and adjacency requirements
- Drawings of existing conditions
- Drawings identifying the total square footage requirements and building function space
- Documents identifying interior code requirements
- Project schedule and budget
- General graphic drawings and diagrams

The audiences for the presentations are wide ranging and could include representatives of a corporation and not the VIPs. For example, retail buyers or merchandisers, department heads, facility managers, developers, or real estate agents may attend. Be certain to identify who is giving approval to proceed.

ASSET MANAGEMENT INC.
PROGRAM SUMMARY

CATEGORY	SPACE DESCRIPTION	SPACE QUANTITY	USABLE SQUARE FOOTAGE	EXTENDED USABLE PROGRAM
WORKSPACES				
	CFO Office	1	150	150
	Locate away from reception			
	Workstation 8' by 7'	90	65	5,850
	Maintain standard as possible			
	54" maximum panel height; developers need 2 PCs			
	Trading Station	32	75	2,400
	Cluster in groups of four; 4-8 monitors per station			
	Receptionist	1	150	150
	Needs line of sight to elevator lobby			
TOTAL OCCUPIED SPACE		124	440	8,550
ANCILLARY				
	Board Room	1	700	700
	20 seats, must have windows			
	Interior glazing to opaque			
	Large Presentation Room	1	1,400	1,400
	100 seats, subdivide into 3 rooms			
	2 projectors/screens per section			
	Small Meeting Rooms	10	225	2,250
	4-6 seats; PC in each; locate one each near CEO,			
	marketing, administration, and technology			
	Server Room	1	700	700
	Pre-action system; 200 servers/20 racks			
	One hour rated enclosure; electronic security			
	Marketing Production Room	1	400	400
	Needs own copier			
	Waiting Area	2	150	300
	Locate one at reception,			
	one near board room			

Figure 4.3
Presentation documents of program summary, identifying the total square footage requirements and building function space, by Allegro Interior Architecture.

Category	Space Description	Space Quantity	Usable Square Footage	Extended Usable Program
ANCILLARY (CONTINUED)				
	Lunch Room	1	350	350
	2 full refrigerator, 2 microwave, 2 coffeemaker			
	sink, 2 trash, recycle bin, cabinets, beverage cooler			
	Kitchenette	1	100	100
	1/2 refrigerator, sink, microwave			
	Quality Control/Quality Assurance	1	400	400
	Include 2 racks for test equipment			
	Seat 5 people for training			
	Records Storage Room	1	300	300
	Rolling file system; locking			
	Operations File Room	1	120	120
	Lateral files; locking			
	Pre-action Room	1	100	100
	Adjacent to Server Room			
	Service Area	2	13	26
	Include copier, printers, supplies			
	AV Equipment/PC Closet	2	13	26
	Locate adjacent to Presentation Room			
	Shower Room	1	100	100
	Locate away from Reception			
	Client Powder Room	1	75	75
	Locate near Reception Area			
	Meditation Room	1	75	75
	Locate near Reception Area			
	Coat Closets	2	35	70
	One adjacent to Server Room, one opposite end of floor			
	IDF Room	2	13	26
	One adjacent to Server Room, one opposite end of floor			
	Storage Cabinets	6	13	78
	Compliance binders, locate near marketing			
	Files, Lateral	10	13	130
	Locate in common area			
TOTAL ANCILLARY SPACE				7,726
TOTAL PROGRAMMABLE SPACE (OCCUPIED + ANCILLARY)				16,276
Circulation factor at 35% of total usable				8,789
TOTAL USABLE SQUARE FOOTAGE				25,065
Average Rentable Factor of 18%				4,512
TOTAL RENTABLE SQUARE FOOTAGE				29,577

Figure 4.4
This design program summary evolves from information-gathering meetings with the client and is presented as a formal document for approval, by Allegro Interior Architecture.

► "Although we were hired to design all of the interior spaces, we were also hired to give the hotel a personality. Prior to coming on board, the hotel was a beautifully designed building that had no interior 'concept' or personality. Our job was to create a destination that would resonate with the guest. Our mission evolved from pure interior design into a serious branding exercise. Once we settled on the theme of Fashion 26, we then filled in the gaps with each area of the project, building up the brand and developing the story about the location, the district, and how the guest relates and interacts with the hotel and spaces." Glen Coben, Glen & Company

Schematic or Preliminary Design

During this lively ideation phase of a project, the designer develops and evaluates possible solutions for the design of the space based upon the programming information. This includes design concept ideation, plan studies, spatial studies, furniture selection, and finish material selections.

For this reason, several meetings can occur during this process to obtain feedback from the client. Various ideas are oftentimes presented to clients to give them a chance to convey their wishes or participate in the process. Once the design team has explored all options and established a clear conceptual direction for the project, these recommendations are presented to the client. The documents for a formal presentation meeting during this phase could include:

- Preliminary Functional Relationships
  - ► Bubble diagrams
  - ► Zoning diagrams
- Preliminary Plans and Designs
  - ► Drawings in the form of plans and sketches
  - ► Elevations, orthographic drawings, sketches to explain concepts

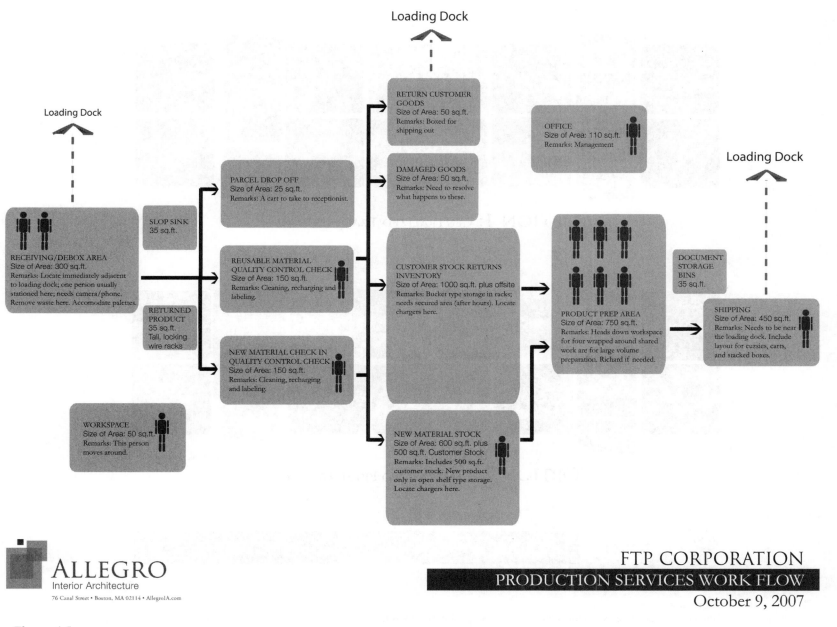

Loading Dock

Loading Dock

Loading Dock

RETURN CUSTOMER GOODS
Size of Area: 50 sq.ft.
Remarks: Boxed for shipping out

OFFICE
Size of Area: 110 sq.ft.
Remarks: Management

PARCEL DROP OFF
Size of Area: 25 sq.ft.
Remarks: A cart to take to receptionist.

DAMAGED GOODS
Size of Area: 50 sq.ft.
Remarks: Need to resolve what happens to these.

SLOP SINK
35 sq.ft.

RECEIVING/DEBOX AREA
Size of Area: 300 sq.ft.
Remarks: Locate immediately adjacent to loading dock; one person usually stationed here; needs camera/phone. Remove waste here. Accomodate palettes.

REUSABLE MATERIAL QUALITY CONTROL CHECK
Size of Area: 150 sq.ft.
Remarks: Cleaning, recharging and labeling.

CUSTOMER STOCK RETURNS INVENTORY
Size of Area: 1000 sq.ft. plus offsite
Remarks: Bucket type storage in racks; needs secured area (after hours). Locate chargers here.

DOCUMENT STORAGE BINS
35 sq.ft.

PRODUCT PREP AREA
Size of Area: 750 sq.ft.
Remarks: Heads down workspace for four wrapped around shared work are for large volume preparation. Richard if needed.

SHIPPING
Size of Area: 450 sq.ft.
Remarks: Needs to be near the loading dock. Include layout for cuzsies, carts, and stacked boxes.

RETURNED PRODUCT
35 sq.ft.
Tall, locking wire racks

NEW MATERIAL CHECK IN QUALITY CONTROL CHECK
Size of Area: 150 sq.ft.
Remarks: Cleaning, recharging and labeling.

WORKSPACE
Size of Area: 50 sq.ft.
Remarks: This person moves around.

NEW MATERIAL STOCK
Size of Area: 600 sq.ft. plus 500 sq.ft. Customer Stock
Remarks: Includes 500 sq.ft. customer stock. New product only in open shelf type storage. Locate chargers here.

ALLEGRO
Interior Architecture
76 Canal Street • Boston, MA 02114 • AllegroIA.com

FTP CORPORATION
PRODUCTION SERVICES WORK FLOW
October 9, 2007

Figure 4.5
Presentation documents of workflow diagram by Allegro Interior Architecture.

INTENTION AND CONTEXT OF PRESENTATION

OPTION 1: CENTRALIZED TRADING ROOM

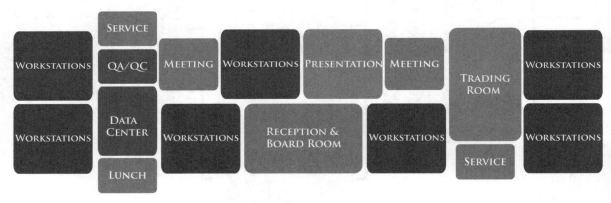

OPTION 2: CENTRALIZED PRESENTATION

Figure 4.6
Presentation documents of bubble diagrams by Allegro Interior Architecture.

- ‣ High profile areas presented in additional detail
- ‣ Suggestions for furniture and finishes in a loose format
- Documentation or drawings explaining
  - ‣ Codes
  - ‣ Building systems
  - ‣ Sustainability
  - ‣ Security
- Budget Documents

The approval meetings for large projects are sequenced in the steps as outlined above. For smaller projects, preliminary plans and spatial concept design are often combined in one presentation meeting. Designers sometimes show the ideas that they reasoned unfavorable before showing their recommended solutions. It is a way of leading the client to the best solution. Alternatively, you may decide to show more than one excellent solution and let the client decide. Either way builds a spirit of teamwork and collaboration. The client is more likely to approve during the next phase because they were part of the decision now. For examples of presentation documents, see Color Plates 1 through 5.

> ▶ "Come to the table with one great design option, and another great one in your back pocket. Bringing five options to the table suggests a lack of conviction and inevitably leads to confusion for both the client and the team." Caleb Mulvena, Mapos, LLC

> ▶ *Slowness of Design.* "So, the first intuitive drawings are usually very rough plan forms which might demonstrate the gesture of the body's movement and how that is expressed by a mass in relationship to the land. We always show these drawings to the client because we want them to understand the intuition or gesture that is the genesis of the design. It is also a way of saying 'I don't know what I am doing yet, but I do have a feeling about it.' " Tod Williams and Billie Tsien, architects

Design Development or Final Design

Based upon the client's approval in the previous phase, the project is refined and completed for final presentation to the client. All designs must comply with building, safety, and accessibility codes and regulations. The documents apply sustainability requirements as well. The final design presentation includes as many visual materials as required to clearly demonstrate and communicate the solution. This list will include any number of plans, elevations, sections, details, orthographic drawings, illustrations or renderings, furniture selections, material selections, models, mock-ups, full-scale furniture samples, and budgets. The plans also may include:

- A floor plan indicating any special design elements and attached interior fixtures keyed to details, sections, and elevations as required
- A furniture plan related to legends, or furniture selections, and materials as required
- A floor-covering plan related to material samples as required
- A reflected ceiling plan indicating ceiling conditions, materials, and any special design elements keyed to details, sections, and elevations as required
- A lighting plan keyed to lighting fixtures

In short, include what can support the communication of your ideas. It is your obligation to include information the client must approve before moving to the next phase of the project. For examples of final presentation documents, see Color Plates 6 through 24. (Color Plates 13 through 24 will be revisited in Chapter 5.)

Construction Documents

The interior construction document phase includes the detailed working drawings that define the work to be constructed. These may include partition plans, power and communications plans, reflected ceiling plans, material and finishes plans, and furniture layout plans, as well as elevations, sections, and details, along with the drawings of associated consultants.[7]

Furniture, fixtures, and equipment (FF&E) specifications, bid documents, vendor coordination, critical path schedules, and installation requirements are also completed in this phase. Interior designers prepare drawings only in accordance with their legal capacity. Architects, engineers, or other consultants may be involved in the coordination and completion of the construction documents. The same is true for issue of bid documents, analysis of bids, and contract awards. Formal presentations are not a requirement during this phase, however, formal meetings are. Significant issues, such as financial and time resources, are reviewed and finalized in these meetings; therefore, thorough preparation and a professional approach are essential.

Design Administration or Contract Administration

During this phase, the interior designer will negotiate furniture pricing, place and track orders, approve samples or strike-offs, review and approve shop drawings, complete finalized furniture installation plans, conduct site visits, coordinate with vendors and contractors, monitor schedules, manage change orders, and schedule installations and deliveries. These tasks are restricted in some geographic locations and may require a contactor's license for project site supervision.

During this phase, a designer will consult with the client as needed to expedite the construction and purchasing for the project. Construction administration meetings, informal meetings with vendors, telephone conversations, electronic submissions of documents, project manager meetings, and job site meetings are examples of contact with the client and others involved in the project.

Although presentations are not required during this phase, meetings are, and the client must approve documents. A professional designer is as prepared for these meeting as if they *were* formal presentations, has on hand all the necessary documents, and is prepared to discuss any issues that might arise. Documents that require client approval include:

- Purchasing proposals
- Invoices for purchases
- Bid proposals
- Change orders

Team Practice

A team approach is the typical way of working in a design office, and in many cases, the team creates and performs the design presentation. The team leader may be the principal of the firm or a senior level designer. The leader sets the direction for the project and collaborates with the design staff assigned to the project. This staff may include expertise in research, codes, planning, spatial design, finishes, lighting, and so on. The team joins both junior and senior designers and explores a wide array of ideas in order to develop a shared vision for a successful project. "In a collaborative effort, it is understood that different points of view add richness and depth to the project, but this means that ego must take a back seat," suggests Scott Simpson of KlingStubbins.[8] The same is true for student critiques.

A written presentation brief is useful in planning a presentation and keeping everyone on the same page. A brief is a written document to help you keep your intentions clear throughout all of the preparations. It is short and to the point and states the presentation intentions, key messages, and to whom these messages are targeted. This brief includes the client's key business initiatives or drivers combined with your analysis of the client. Alan Dandron, principal of Mancini Duffy, believes that:

> Design solutions are the direct result of responding to a client's core business drivers. Before design even begins, we seek to understand our client's firm culture and organizational attributes; we also seek to understand what makes them "special." This knowledge helps us create a design that responds to their culture, organizational attributes, and specific project business drivers.[9]

Regardless of the purpose of your presentation—to persuade or inform—your intentions must be clear from the start in order to effectively present and communicate during any phase of a design project.

▶ "In a team setting, it's critical to clearly establish not only which team member is responsible for delivery of which component of the presentation, but to agree upon the transition or 'hand-off' between presenters. This will further convey to the client/audience that your team works well together, which is often a primary consideration when awarding the contract for a project." John R. Sadlon, managing principal at Mancini Duffy

▶ "We like to think of our work as 'brand poetry,' or an artistic solution for commercial needs. Artistic solutions target emotions; emotions connect people in a meaningful way. Emotive experiences attract more people to them, and engage them longer." UXUS Design

Dialogue with Peter Joehnk

JOI-Design
Peter Joehnk, and Corinna Kretschmar-Joehnk, Principals

Q. Do you have an ideological basis for your design work? How does this integrate with your client presentation method?

A. JOI-Design works according to the motto: Interior design is three-dimensional marketing, so we are not ideological, but we try to react to the needs of our client (and his clients). This philosophy is part of our presentation, as we always explain first, why the design looks like it looks.

Q. In preparation for presenting the final design, what method do you use for going over the project? Do you sit down with your team and draw the details of the design concept out of them, or do you set the idea and then explore it with your design team?

A. As we are a relatively big office, [the two of us] make the first contact with the client [and] develop the general idea for a design concept, which then is developed by our team. We then "filter" the new ideas and sometimes adjust directions, and, of course, check in-between to see what the result will look like.[10]

Idea Exchange

Watch the following videos and then discuss and compare the views expressed with your design colleagues:

- NRDC Artists & Visionaries: Jeanne Gang, Architect. www .di.net/videos/3401/.
- Michael Vanderbyl, Principal, Vanderbyl Design, San Francisco. Design Thinking Out Loud: Jack of All Trades v Master of One. www.youtube.com/watch?v=eG3VIxHijuE.
- Timothy Brown, Innovation Through Design Thinking, March 16, 2006. Running Time: 57:17. http://mitworld.mit .edu/video/357.
- Tim Brown urges designers to think big. http://www.ted .com/talks/tim_brown_urges_designers_to_think_big.html.
- Tim Brown on creativity and play. http://www.ted.com/ talks/tim_brown_on_creativity_and_play.html.

Create Experience

Discussion

Speaking one at a time, group members answer one of these questions: What do you think a final design presentation should accomplish? What is the role of the designer in the community?

Debate

Watch the video "Arts.21 | When Is Design Art, and When Is Art Design?" at DesignIntelligence (http://www.di.net/ videos/3069/). Debate your position regarding the value of design as art.

Setting Objectives

Personal Objectives. In this course I wish to:

Presentation Objectives. My objectives for this presentation are:

Presentation Brief

Write a brief using an existing project as assigned by your instructor.

Part 1 Who

Who is the client? Who are the end users? Who are the viewers?

Who is presenting?

Part 2 What

What is the key message of the presentation?

Part 3 Why

Why does the client want a design solution?

Part 4 Where

Where is the presentation?

Part 5 When

When is the presentation date?

Part 6 How

How will you implement the presentation solution? (Media: print, video, slides, Web; and budget.)

5 Presentation Development

We have been working with the noted chef/neurologist from Barcelona, Dr. Miguel Sánchez Romera, on his first restaurant in New York City. We have been working together for close to two years on the design, and in this time, I have spent time with Miguel in his kitchen in Barcelona, with him at the Bouqueria shopping for food, and hanging out with him. The process has been amazing—translating his culinary vision into a series of rooms, which communicate the essence of Miguel. The process has been inspirational. The only challenge was the fact that at the beginning, Miguel didn't speak English and I didn't speak Spanish. We communicated through drawings, sketches, and photographs, which allowed us to be very clear in what we were doing.[1]

— Glen Coben, Glen & Company

Coben's challenge sounds exhilarating and a bit like playing *Win, Lose or Draw*. The first significant point is that he communicated the essence of Miguel. The second is how his visuals brought clarity to their message. As designers, we are fortunate to have visuals as reference to begin our storytelling. In Coben's case, they are necessary, and no doubt appreciated by Romera, also a talented visual artist. His culinary enchantments are designed to engage the senses and consequently induce our memories. A refined design presentation, like Romera's approach (culinary constructionism) to cooking and eating, takes considerable planning.

Structure of a Presentation

Once the analysis of the client and presentation goal has been established, you are ready to decide on a presentation approach. First, several organizational tasks need to be completed, regardless of whether the presentation is a solo or team effort. The preparation for a design presentation involves all design team members coming together with the same purpose and goal for the best outcome. Alan Dandron explains that the Mancini Duffy teams:

> . . . have an internal team meeting to review the goals for the project and discuss the design. This approach allows us to set a general direction for the design that the entire design team can then follow, which means that the team is then designing to the same goal and is much more efficient. The team's ideas are reviewed and we then refine them for the presentation—an approach that allows the members of the team to have ownership of the design and creates a better result.[2]

We will focus on a final design presentation in this chapter. Chapter 4 includes discussion about preliminary phase presentations and other concerns.

Visuals are essential for an interior design presentation at any stage, and the outcome of your presentation counts on first-rate preparation. A viewer should be able to extract your message from the visuals alone in a well-organized and thoroughly prepared presentation such as the Chemistree presentation by Kristyn Hill shown in Color Plates 13 through 24. As you know, this is a large amount of information to organize, prepare, and present. If you find that the visuals are not up to par, lack clarity, or do not solve the design problem when you are preparing the oral delivery, it is time to go back to the drawing board for more analysis.

Most designers agree that many clients do not have the ability to understand floor plans and elevations. This is why it is important to communicate with 3-D views of the spaces and, as Alan Dandron suggests, "make references to spaces they are familiar with" when discussing a plan. He adds, "This helps them understand the size and scale of spaces."[3] Similarly, Vicente Wolfe believes it is important to explain the space and "build a picture in their minds."[4]

In some cases, the presentation may have a limited number of visuals. This can occur when the contract specifically outlines the limits of the presentation documents or excludes a specific document. For instance, a rendering or 3-D video animation is costly to produce, so the designer includes it as a reimbursable expense to reduce overall design fees for the client. This gives the client an option to request the illustration as an additional expenditure if they feel that they need it to make a decision or to use as a marketing tool for the project. (Refer to how contracts influence presentations in Chapter 4.)

Smart design team managers use the unique skills of their individual team members. As thoughtfully stated by John R. Sadlon of Mancini Duffy:

It's important to not only determine the best presentation style for the company you're pitching to but to uncover the best methods for your team, and each individual within it. When considering your approach, it's advantageous to establish guidelines to streamline both the preparation for and the delivery of a presentation. These guidelines should be flexible and easily adapted to address the unique requirements of a particular client or presentation, since it's unlikely that one fixed approach will work for all presentations.[5]

▶ "We usually try to find the story, which is different [from] the story of [the] competing projects around. So the analysis of the situation is the start for design and presentation." Peter Joehnk, principal at JOI-Design

Organization and Preparation

Marcel Wanders says, "Unlike product design, interiors are about theater. They lead you from one idea to the next and the next."[6] Likewise, we organize an appropriate sequence for the experience by using spatial order. Unique interior spaces are discussed one at a time. You also need to plan transitions in order for the client to follow the organization. This is easy for a designer because habitable spaces have divisions and classifications. Interiors have logical entry points, direction of movement, transition points, and often several levels. They also have zones, including public or social, working, and private. Interior spaces also have areas of emphasis with unique features for special focus. These are great help in determining where to start and where to transition within the presentation's core segment. Achieve flow with logical links between sections or segments and associate them to the main concept.

Additionally, some designers divide the presentation into parts. If a project team is presenting, sometimes the segments are divided among the team by way of their project responsibilities—planning, design, or lighting, for instance. These sections do have a logical design process category.

Visuals

The dimensional graphics used for a design presentation have the same purpose whether they are hand drawn or computerized visuals. Their purpose is helping the viewers visualize the design attributes and navigate unfamiliar spatial territory. We use three basic methods to show spatial information in a presentation:

- 2-D plan, elevation, and section views (Color Plate 25)
- 3-D immersion and encapsulated views (Color Plate 26)
- 3-D models (Color Plate 27)

◀ 65 ▶

A plan contains a comprehensive overview of information about the space but limits our grasp of the realistic conditions of the spatial environment. Elevations and sections give more information but also limit understanding of the detailed surroundings. 3-D views and models allow the viewer to see more of the spatial relationships and their complexities. The higher and wider the viewpoints in 3-D views, the fewer details are communicated. When the field of view is near or within the space, close to the reality of actual space, the viewer has a more immersive experience of the space and is able to see more of the details. The benefits of computerized animated immersive views are the ability to rotate the viewpoint to see the complete space and the interaction of walking around within it. Without computer animation, the static multiple viewpoints of immersive spatial illustrations combined with plans and elevations convey enough tiers of information to the viewer to comprehend the details. Designers also layer information, which is viewed in separate plans to indicate floor covering solutions and details, ceiling and lighting conditions, and power requirements, for example.

Layout

The complex task is how to integrate multiple visuals at one time when presenting each individual space of the interior. The most striking design feature should be the dominant focal point within a 3-D visual to make the greatest impression on the viewer. For example, a hotel lobby water feature or registration area will be more striking than the entry vestibule or interior valet area. Many designers begin a presentation with the most striking visual. In laying out the individual slides or boards of a presentation, you have the task of planning layouts in order to lead the viewer's eye to specific areas in a sequence. Additionally, you must develop a predetermined order of structure and content.

You may also decide to initiate connection with your viewers by using a vivid opening visual, placing it in eyesight as they begin to gather into the presentation space. The visual may be a slide image, design board, or item on the conference table. If the slide or object is viewable while people enter the meeting room, it will arouse curiosity, motivate interest, and immediately involve everyone in the presentation. Let's suppose your design concept is metamorphic in some way—representing change. Add a bit of drama with an image of a large metamorphic rock on a screen or a small bowl at each seat filled with crushed quartzite and marble. Oh, the suspense—they *will* be focused! Open with a story related to the process of transformation, change in form, layering, and crystallization of the metamorphic rock. Point to the contents of the bowls and invite them to explore the texture, color, and shapes. Next, begin to relate the transformation and change of the client's environment through the new design viewers will see in a few minutes. Of course, add a bit of drama to your metamorphic prologue. This makes a presentation memorable. In short, do not be afraid to influence the way your viewers take in and act in response to the design and presentation.

At the same time, be careful with multi-image visuals. We cannot expect the viewer to build an elaborate mental map of the project in a presentation. Single boards or slides consisting of a rendered plan, section, rendered elevation, rendered perspective, furniture images, and materials are potentially distracting. It is our job to use Gestalt principles and lay out the visuals to direct the eyes to specific areas. The arrangement methods used to group the elements, as well as the use of white space (or negative space), has a great influence. Normally the eye goes to a visual image before text; however, size, style, and color are used to create dominance and hierarchy for visuals and text. See Figures 5.1 through 5.4. The principles of visual organization are utilized to achieve the best results.

Professional designers also unify the diverse visual segments of a presentation with graphics or text. Presentation visuals have one font set throughout and up to two complementary fonts. Like a Web page or PowerPoint slide, the presentation must have a unifying *skin*. This gives the illusion that the viewer is always in the same visual space. Great presentation graphics utilize sound, basic design principles of arrangement, and the Gestalt principles of organization and grouping. Make it a better experience for the viewer by using the principles of alignment, closure, similarity, proximity, and continuity. Group together the conceptually related elements of a slide (Figures 5.5 and 5.6). Your presentation is a visual graphic—design it well! In the book *Design Portfolios*, Diane Bender explains related elements this way: "An underlying concept that is consistently demonstrated in the way you arrange your work or add additional graphic elements." By doing this for every presentation, you can be ahead of the game of preparing your work portfolio.

Furthermore, schedules, checklists, whiteboards, paper rolls, Post-its, and storyboards are useful tools to help you plan what to include and subsequently prepare the oral content. Consequently, use these tools well in advance to allow you to try out presentation ideas, plan

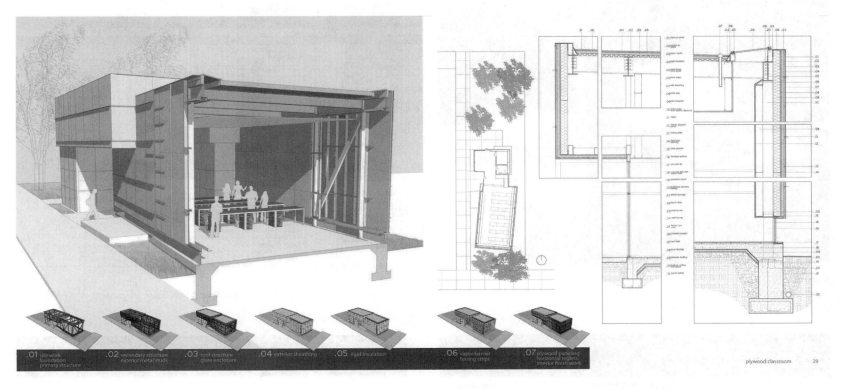

Figure 5.1
Sample board layouts from the portfolio of Christopher Flass. The dominant visual is the 3-D illustration, and the viewer will focus on it first. If the additional illustrations in this layout were full color, they would compete for our attention. The graphics at the lower edge are the unifying design element, extending to the right side to connect both pages.

the visuals needed, and develop the flow. Using these methods to prepare will help you see the whole picture and develop clarity for the oral content. All of these elements are prepared well in advance of the final presentation. Use them to organize and prepare your oral presentation delivery.

▶ "We (designers) are trained to make images, animations, or objects that evoke emotions and interactions. So it is only natural that we take advantage of our skills to make people see, hear, and touch our research as well." Qin Han, PhD., Service Design and Design Management

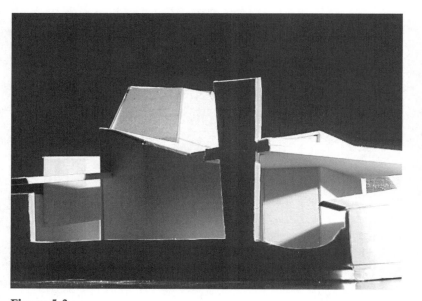

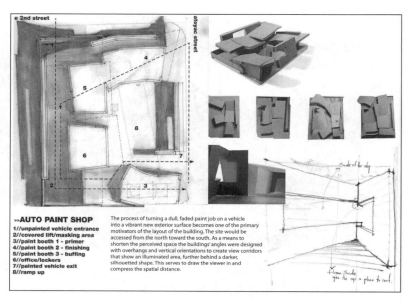

>>AUTO PAINT SHOP
1//unpainted vehicle entrance
2//covered lift/masking area
3//paint booth 1 - primer
4//paint booth 2 - finishing
5//paint booth 3 - buffing
6//office/lockers
7//painted vehicle exit
8//ramp up

The process of turning a dull, faded paint job on a vehicle into a vibrant new exterior surface becomes one of the primary motivators of the layout of the building. The site would be accessed from the north toward the south. As a means to shorten the perceived space the buildings' angles were designed with overhangs and vertical orientations to create view corridors that show an illuminated area, further behind a darker, silhouetted shape. This serves to draw the viewer in and compress the spatial distance.

Figure 5.2

Sample board layouts from the portfolio of John Locke. Size, style, and color are used to create dominance and hierarchy for visuals and text. Edge alignment is used to group dissimilar items and related items.

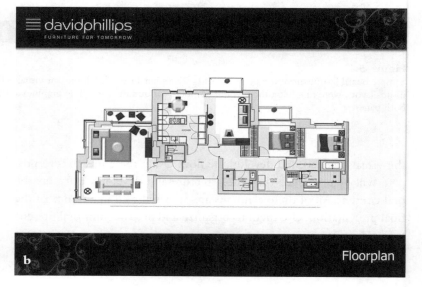

Figure 5.3
Sample board layouts by David Phillips, interior designer. The logo and room identification are dominant text with smaller text identifying room design elements. Unlike objects, shapes, and materials are organized in order to align horizontally and are visually anchored within the horizontal lines (a). Bold geometric and curvilinear graphics and text unify the presentation boards (b).

(re)presentation

object | content | *expression*

Figure 5.4
Sample board layouts from the portfolio of
Dalen Gilbrech. Text size hierarchy and use of
white space directs the eye from left to right
before the viewer will focus on the visuals. In
this case, the text leads the viewer to the visuals.

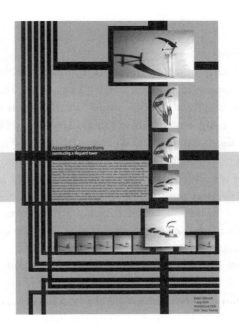

lifeguard tower
assembling connections

The lifeguard tower concept was all
about connectivity; the connection of
building elements, connectivity to
the site, between beach-goers and
lifeguards and the inherent connection between humans and nature.
Hence, in order to represent this
project in a visual display I used the
intersection of lines, the strands of
the project, as the site of milestone
images in the development of the
building concept and design.

Figure 5.5
Presentation visuals may be set up with the plan on the table surface and
illustrations with material samples on a wall surface or easel.

Figure 5.6
Alternate presentation layouts include grouping a plan segment with the
illustrations and material samples. This may be presented on the table, wall, easel,
or slide projection.

Storyboards

Prepared early in the design process, storyboards help you block out a presentation; again, think of theater. They help visualize the project and presentation, provide opportunities for discussion and refinement, and help you budget materials, resources, and time. The storyboard technique is also useful to study what you might say while engaging the audience. The concept is your broad theme or central idea. The collective whole of the entire space tells this story. The story, in turn, finds expression and support through the specific details and features you tell about the space. The visuals enable the client to see what you are explaining. Remember that the viewers should take away the concept message after the presentation.

Each visual group will have several statements that make it significant. These are your primary messages to justify the concept. Figures 5.7 and 5.8 illustrate this process using a storybook page technique. The descriptions should be orderly and do not have to include every detail. Focus on the details that support the concept. Arrange the details to create a clear picture in the mind of the viewer. Answer the questions shown in Figure 5.7 to determine what the important dialogue might be.

John R. Sadlon, managing principal at Mancini Duffy, goes on to say:

> In addition to a well-executed design solution, analysis and research are also critical to the delivery of a successful design presentation. It is important to identify each primary component of the presentation, and to formulate a strategy that ensures appropriate time to prepare the materials and create an appropriate message to ensure your success. Storyboards are a fundamental tool that should be used early-on in the process and updated regularly throughout the evolution of your work.[7]

It is up to you and the design team to judge the relevance of every item in the space and whether or not it supports your message. Material that is relevant to the operational needs of the space but not central enough for inclusion in a design presentation (height of a counter, for example) may not be pointed out; however, be prepared to discuss all issues and features. Secondary and tertiary points or information also exist in a design solution. A secondary point intertwines important information into the primary concept. Secondary points are eliminated if you know the viewer is not interested. If so, secondary points are communicated with a note on the plans or presentation visuals. Tertiary points are those that are not necessary to include in the presentation. If there is enough time and they enhance the presentation, you can consider including them. An example of a tertiary point might be an interesting piece of information about solving the design problem, a product, or manufacturer that you want to share with the viewers. It usually is not necessary to include all manufacturer details in a design presentation because those details are communicated in the construction documents. Be flexible when analyzing what is to be included or excluded. Throw it out if it is not relevant.

▶ As with any design, "It's always about the editing, learning how to cut things out and how to pare away. . . . From my younger self and from my teaching, I know just how hard that is. Because when you're less experienced, you hold on to everything. You're so proud to have had these ideas, you can't bear to let even one go." Romilly Saumarez Smith, artist

▶ Do review the changes from the previous presentation. Briefly, discuss how you have solved the issue. Use a collaborative style by saying, "Your observation led to a better solution. Thank you, we are glad you caught this." Ownership and allies lead to support for final approval.

ENTICE

OPENING STATEMENT

Write out the opening statement here.

ENGAGE

ENGAGE VISUAL

Paste a copy of your visual here. This helps
remind you of what to include in the narration.
This visual is a duplicate of a presentation board,
PowerPoint slide, digital image, still shot, video
clip, sketch, graphic, or other visual that will
appear before the viewer.

A larger or full size copy should be nearby
in order to write the appropriate narration.

ENGAGE NARRATION

Write out your descriptive and supporting dialogue for
the visual here. Questions to determine important
dialogue are:

How do the details tie into the design concept?
How has it solved the specific program requirements?
What are the most important items to clarify?
What are the dynamic features?
What are the specific details of the
        Plan solution
        Floor covering
        Ceiling
        Lighting solution
        Finish selections
        Furniture selection
        Material selections
What revisions were made since the previous
presentation?

EQUATE

EQUATE CLOSING STATEMENT

Write out the closing statement here.

MEDIA

List the specific visual or audio media
needs.

CONCEPT STATEMENT

Write out the concept statement here. It serves to remind
you of the design intent and keeps the narration focused.

PROJECT NAME

DATE

PAGE __ OF __

Write out the page,
slide, or screen number
for the presentation in
sequence here.

Figure 5.7
Storyboard diagram with prompt questions.

ENTICE   OPENING STATEMENT

....

ENGAGE   ENGAGE VISUAL   ENGAGE NARRATION

Essential ideas:

1. _____
    a. – – – – – – – – – – – – – – – –
    b. – – – – – – – – – – – – – – – –
    c. – – – – – – – – – – – – – – – –
        i. ....
        ii. ....

2. _____
    a. – – – – – – – – – – – – – – – –
        i. ....
        ii. ....
        iii. ....
    b. – – – – – – – – – – – – – – – –
    c. – – – – – – – – – – – – – – – –

3. _____
    a. – – – – – – – – – – – – – – – –
    b. – – – – – – – – – – – – – – – –
    c. – – – – – – – – – – – – – – – –
        i. ....
        ii. ....

....

EQUATE   EQUATE CLOSING STATEMENT   MEDIA

....

CONCEPT STATEMENT

....

PROJECT NAME   **DATE**   **PAGE ___ OF ___**

Figure 5.8
Storyboard diagram with project images inserted. Experiment with your narration and develop the ideas for a design presentation. Pin them up and brainstorm those ideas with the design team.

After determining what details to include, develop a persuasive oral content for each visual based on techniques discussed in Chapter 1. Present your descriptions and details in order to support the right impression for the viewer. The answers to those questions listed in Figure 5.7 are what you will include in your talk. Number them in the order that you want to talk about them. Now decide what to keep and what to eliminate or to address through one of the other visuals. Select the details that add to the viewers' understanding, and eliminate irrelevant ones from the portrayal you are trying to emphasize. Write this in full sentences and later reduce it to key points for a presentation slide, notes, cue cards, or marketing text file.

Moreover, you may also need to make slight changes during the presentation itself. Peter Joehnk of JOI-Design is able to recognize the emotions of his clients and offers this advice: "During most of the presentation, you can see the perception of the words you say and the things you show in the faces of your clients. This can be positive or negative, and you should either strengthen this point, or let it fall."[8]

Now decide what impression your dialogue makes on the viewer. Is the mood of the concept evident? Does the presentation prove the concept statement? Have you expressed the details with clarity? Have you developed the right mixture of strategies to engage the viewer? Check for oversimplified, overembellished, or monotonous segments. Make clear detailed notes and review them several times—it will help you to know your material.

> ▶ Always begin the sequence with the first space observed when entering the primary entrance of a building, regardless of the number of floors in the building.

Next, plan for transitions to establish a flow for the presentation and tie elements together. If you have divided and classified the material in an orderly way, the transitions will be logical. Tim Brown calls it an "emotional blueprint that captures how people travel through the experience in time and turns the most meaningful points into opportunities."[9] Figure 5.9 indicates a few logical spatial transition points.

Before you rehearse, be certain to review and identify the weak points. Refer to your audience analysis and identify those who might oppose and those who are neutral. Likewise, consider the questions they might ask. Do you have appropriate replies prepared?

> ▶ Healthcare clients understand numbers, figures, and return on investment. Thus, the most positive response may result from a designer who delivers measurable impact that is evidence-based. Design solutions are more likely to be justified when communicated in terms that make sense to hospital administrators.

Rehearsal

John R. Sadlon of Mancini Duffy makes the following recommendations, which are expanded upon in the Create Experience section at the end of this chapter:

> It's always advantageous to rehearse at key stages before delivering a presentation as a means to ensure your ability to concisely articulate a message to your client that reinforces your primary design objectives. This is even more imperative when presenting as part of a group, when each team member's speaking points are ideally conveyed in a manner that is balanced, consistent, and supportive of the other team members' speaking points.[10]

BUILDING ORGANIZATION

Building module and level changes.
Begin with first level or entry level. Proceed to upper levels. The elevator lobby or core is the starting location within this floor plan.

SPATIAL SEQUENCE OF EXPERIENCE

A bank, theater, or restaurant would be presented based upon the sequence of events experienced by the end user. Create a "customer journey" that describes the travel process as a positive interaction.[11]

SPATIAL TIMELINES

For example, a museum or gallery exhibit may have a spatial timeline experience.

SPATIAL BOUNDARIES

The boundaries may be closed or open. For instance the enclosed private offices are separated from the open work spaces. The reception is open to the waiting area therefore the transition occurs between the two spaces. Circulation or passage space are transition areas.

ZONES OF A SPACE

Homes include social, utility, and private zones. A zone may also be modular or departmental units. Commercial spaces have a service zone, public zone, semi-private zone, and private (staff) zone.

PRIVATE

SEMI-PRIVATE

PUBLIC

MATERIAL CHANGE

Location of a material where it either stops or continues into another space. For example, the floor covering material.

DESIGN FEATURES

Design elements such as a ceiling condition or change in height. Does the design element end in a particular space or is it a flowing or repetitive element leading to an adjacent space?

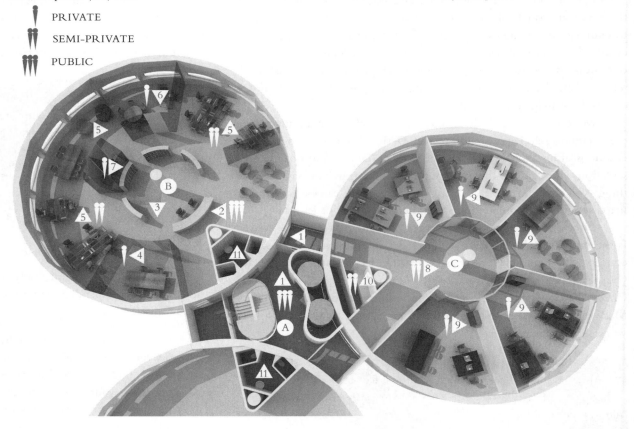

Figure 5.9

Diagram noting the areas of an interior space to use as possible transitions in a design presentation. Use visual thinking to plan the sequence and transitions. Use your floor plans, identify your plan sequence and transition areas, and mark them on your floor plan.

The best plan for your oral delivery is to carefully prepare well in advance but to deliver the actual presentation without notes. Reading from a script or memorizing word for word does not engage a listener, regardless of the wonderful design or descriptions of it. After you have a well-developed outline and notes for your presentation, including opening, core, and closing, practice your presentation with the visuals. Some professionals advise condensing the message to the key message per visual to help gain clarity. You can put your message through the Twitter test of 140 characters per visual. In the actual presentation, you are not limited to 140 characters, but this can help you know your key points and make you a better presenter.

Imaging

Your first practice can be done alone, in front of your peers, or in a video recording. Practice aloud, paying attention to how you speak, what you emphasize, and where you pause. Practice making eye contact with everyone. Be sure you stand, and project your voice as well as observe your tone of voice, posture, and body language. These, well placed, are signals to the viewers that you are emphasizing a particular design feature or making a transition between major points of the design solution. Gestures—hand, body, and facial—add interest. Voice pitch can be raised and lowered to avoid boring the viewers. Use pauses for emphasis or to allow the viewer to absorb and consider the information presented—plan them well. Observe where you need improvements as you practice and correct problem areas.

Subsequent rehearsals are in front of your peers or a trusted family member or friend. You will need their comments to make improvements. Ask for feedback on your voice, rhythm, language use, and your body posture and language. If you are not confident enough to practice in front of them, you are certainly not ready for your presentation. In that case, use a mirror or video-record yourself until you are ready. Check that you made good eye contact, were on your mark, used a clear voice, and pronounced all vocabulary well. Finally, if you plan to wear new shoes or a garment that you have not worn to a presentation before, practice while wearing it. Chapter 10 deals with the reason behind this advice.

▶ Do control timing and flow of presentation with scheduled breaks for a presentation of long duration. Otherwise, you run the risk of unwanted interruptions, distractions, missed information, and loss of focus and attention.

It's All in the Timing

While most design presentations are not restricted to a time limit, student presentations typically are. In either case, time yourself during the last practice session. Make adjustments to meet your time limits and to plan breaks for long presentations. Rehearsing your presentations using a PechaKucha format is a helpful way to gain proficiency within a limited time allowance. PechaKucha 20x20 is a simple presentation format that involves showing 20 images, each for 20 seconds. PechaKucha was devised by Astrid Klein and Mark Dytham and their office Klein Dytham architecture. Keep the presentation of a short duration if it is feasible, but do not sacrifice content and do not rush. Incomplete presentations are not justified to shorten the time of a professional or student presentation. Any presentation that is over 60 minutes needs a short break planned into the delivery. This gives the viewers an opportunity to absorb the information presented, clear their thoughts to receive more, and keep the goals on target at the same time.

Do not allow the break time to lead the presentation in a conflicting direction. Natural break points are the clear transitions between levels of a space or zones of a space, for example. An increase in the amount of coughing or fidgeting from the viewers is a sign to wrap up that part of the presentation and move on or take a break. A break for refreshments, conversations, or a trip to the restroom before moving on to the balance of the presentation is often welcome during lengthy meetings. Plan what you will say and do during the break and control the time limit of the break.

Remember, your viewers will interact with questions, suggestions, and objections. You will not be able to eliminate questions or objections, but you will be able to answer them intelligently if you prepare. Professional speakers, politicians, and students rehearse for these moments with colleagues and peers acting as the audience. Do the same by asking your rehearsal audience to ask questions or challenge ideas. This allows you to prepare your responses or, if needed, refine your presentation. Chapter 7 includes collaboration techniques to address objections with appropriate and knowledgeable replies.

Document

It is professional practice to document presentation notes, text, images, and electronic presentations before any presentation leaves the office. You can use this documentation if originals are destroyed or lost, to create a leave-behind, to practice, to distribute to team members, for later reference when completing construction documents, and for future marketing efforts.

Notes and Cue Cards

Ruffling through notes, papers, and cards during a presentation gives the impression that you do not know your material and are unprofessional. Another drawback with cue cards or notes is that they occupy your hands. Holding papers is distracting and limits your ability to gracefully use a pointer, gesture to indicate a feature on your visual, make a note, or draw graphics on a plan. When you truly know the project and the material you are presenting, you will perform more effectively rather than merely reading from your notes. Nonetheless, always have a text document of your presentation to refer to in the event that someone has to fill in for you. The same is true for a script for any electronic media presentation.

Cue cards may be used to guide you through a relatively small presentation. While organizing the presentation, decide what features you want to highlight, the order in which they will be presented, and make notes on the cards. Prepare them in advance, number each card, and be sure to use large type and only one side of each card. Cue cards may include only key words to help press your memory, or be expanded to include phrases or facts. Again, use the Twitter test for key point reduction to 140 characters. Cue cards are recommended for your rehearsal sessions. Use them until the presentation resides in your memory—not memorized word for word.

Image Documentation

Make a backup set or copy of any electronic media used in the presentation. Unfortunately, not everything goes according to plan and having copies of the presentation in both print and electronic media can save the day. These documents are also a record of the presentation that is used for future reference. That reference may be as simple as recording the project presentation for archives or assisting you and the other team members in producing the construction documents and project books for the project. The documentation must be detailed enough so that another person could continue the work without you. Design presentations are works in progress, and each phase must be documented. You will be grateful to have all the documentation when making changes, preparing a portfolio, or organizing the project for future publication.

Agenda

The best time to schedule a meeting is first thing in the morning before participants are engrossed in other daily work issues. Comprehensive meeting planning includes an agenda, which is a summarization of a meeting, distinct from a presentation agenda. It is distributed to everyone who attends the presentation meeting and gives the viewers an idea of what will occur in the meeting and in what order. Short and simple is best. Include items, in order, that you plan to discuss, approve, or announce in addition to a typical header including: organization name, participants, location, date, and time. It is always good practice to note the break time and question segments. Extend courtesies by introducing newcomers and allowing a short conversation time to allow latecomers to arrive. A presentation meeting agenda also has a very clear objective—to secure the approval from the client to proceed—and the items on your agenda must be directly related to this goal. Alan Dandron, principal at Mancini Duffy, expands this point with this statement:

> There should always be an agenda for a presentation. The agenda should serve as an outline to make sure that all of the points that need to be reviewed are discussed. However, it's always important to be flexible with the client, so if an area is discussed out of order, it's not a problem; the presenter can always steer the conversation back to the agenda points. It's helpful to start the presentation by reviewing the agenda and what you hope to cover. This will help the client understand what needs to be addressed, and help to keep them from jumping ahead in the presentation.[12]

Leave-Behind

Handouts that highlight the presentation can be given to the client after the presentation is complete. Not all of the content of your presentation has to be included in the document. Never give the viewers anything but a printed agenda before the presentation. John Sadlon remarks:

> Frequently overlooked in the early planning process is an item that is commonly referred to as the presentation "leave-behind." Essentially, this is a product or document that you give to the client/audience at the end of your presentation that will serve as a reminder of your presentation. It may be as simple as a CD with images of your work, or it may be something more elaborate. Regardless of the media, it should serve to specifically remind your client of the key message and unique design solution of your presentation.[13]

Gifts and protocol are discussed in Chapter 10.

Designers converse on many levels; however, like Coben and Romera, conversing through drawings, sketches, and photographs allow us to be very clear in what we are doing.

> ▶ "Try to keep the line of the story you want to tell. Don't write the wording of your presentation down, but make yourself aware of some key words that you want to use . . . and stay the person that you really are, be authentic." Peter Joehnk, principal at JOI-Design

> ▶ What advice do you have for young designers in the A&D (architecture and design) field? "Do get a good education from a good school. Do internships. Do not try to go out on your own right away. Respect your own thoughts and ideas, but realize that you need to grow and nourish them to turn them into reality." Lauren Rottet, FAIA, IIDA

Dialogue with John R. Sadlon

Mancini Duffy, New York, New York
John R. Sadlon, Managing Principal

Q. Do you need some sort of physical or mental warm-up before presenting to a client? Are there any do's and don'ts you would recommend?

A. At a minimum, it is advisable to schedule a first rehearsal approximately one week prior to the presentation date and a second rehearsal a day or two before a presentation. The first rehearsal should include a pin-up of all design materials in progress that are intended to be presented, for the purposes of evaluating the state of completion for each deliverable, as well as for strategizing how best to complete each drawing/image in a timely manner. This streamlines the production effort for the final week and helps ensure that all design deliverables are completed to a similar degree of refinement. The first rehearsal is also the time to identify the key concept(s) that you would like to convey to your client and to formulate the strongest possible message to do so. A result of this first rehearsal should be a clear and definitive strategy for completion of all work, as well as articulation of the primary message to be delivered at your presentation.

The second rehearsal should include a pin-up of all design materials in their completed format. This is the point at which design exploration is complete and the focus of preparation should shift from production of the work to crafting your final presentation message. This requires discipline, since there's a strong tendency to want to refine the design up until the last moment before a presentation. It is imperative to leave a sufficient period of time to prepare a professional-level presentation.

To help hone your speaking points, it's often helpful to have a "dress-rehearsal" of your entire presentation with a third party acting in the role of the client. This person can provide valuable feedback regarding the clarity of your message, as well as the efficiency with which it is delivered. It is also helpful to clock the timing of your presentation and to assess how to adjust your speaking points to fit within the time allotted for your presentation.

Do's before a presentation:

- Plan ahead to allow sufficient time for rehearsing your message and finalizing your deliverables.
- Invite the participation of all team members in the first rehearsal so that all have a common understanding of the presentation objectives.
- Invite a third party to your second rehearsal, and encourage their feedback regarding the effectiveness of your presentation approach. Make final adjustments as necessary, based on their comments.[14]

Color Plate 1
Design concept drawing for a sitting room by Albert Hadley. Freehand sketching is often utilized for preliminary presentations to establish the direction for a project. It may be complemented with color and material samples and photographs of furniture.

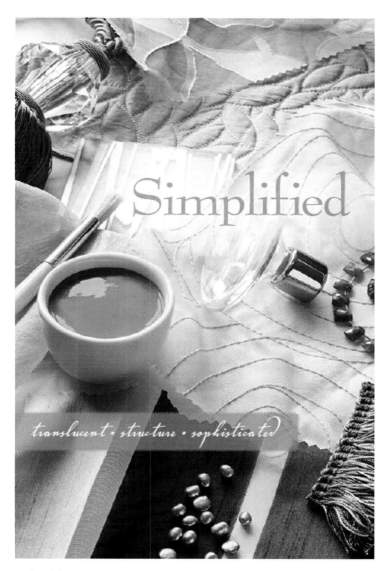

Color Plate 2
Concept board for presentation of interior material samples. An artistic arrangement of unfastened samples is appropriate for preliminary presentations because it sets the attitude and encourages the viewer to feel the qualities of a material.

Color Plate 3
Hotel lobby design concept sketch by Garry Cohn. Preliminary presentations of large projects may include many perspective sketches to illustrate the design details. All illustrations may be without color, loosely colored, important design features colored, or the primary illustration fully colored.

Color Plate 4
Hotel lobby design concept idea board by Garry Cohn. Idea, concept, or mood boards help to further illustrate the project design in a preliminary presentation.

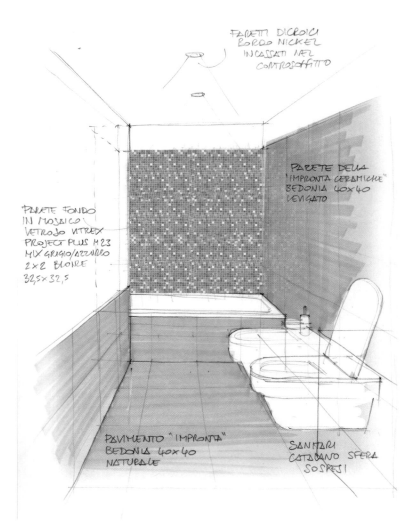

Color Plate 5
Concept sketch of a residential bathroom with color and notations by Franco Bernardini. Sketches with color and notations add clarity and invite discussion. They are also useful to communicate information to a professional illustrator for the final illustration.

Color Plate 6
Final design presentation computer illustration of the same residential bathroom in Color Plate 5 by Roberto De Angelis. Designed by Franco Bernardini.

Color Plate 7
Final design presentation computer illustration of student dining hall as a haven and a habitat, complete with floating clouds made of felt, and falling raindrops. Uni Mensa Hardenbergstrasse by JOI-Design.

Color Plate 8
Nature as the focus of the interior design concept is achieved with an overall bright, earthy, green, and white space. Materials such as wood, leather, and felt contribute to the vision of a naturally grown atmosphere. Final design presentation moodboard (or sample board), with furnishings, color, pattern, and texture, of Uni Mensa Hardenbergstrasse by JOI-Design.

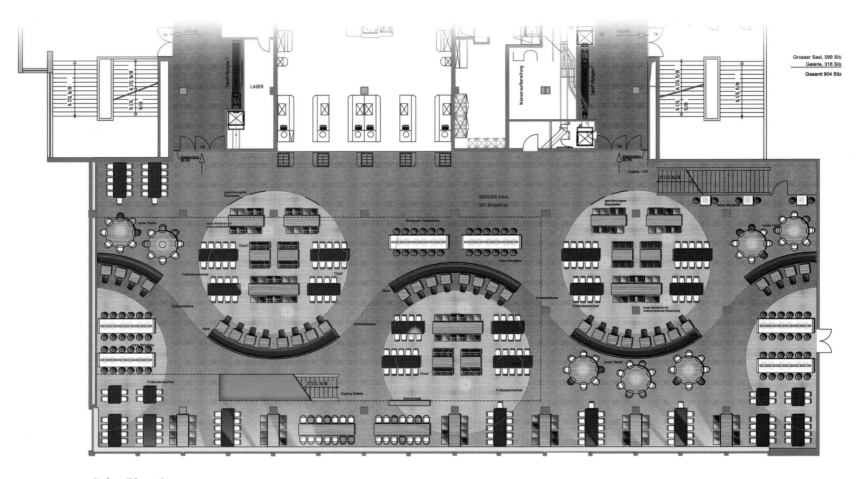

Color Plate 9

The separation of different areas into "islands," each with its own design of chairs and tables, visualizes the idea of nature. The plan and design approach reinforce a café-like atmosphere in a large 16,000-square-foot space. Final design presentation illustrated floor plan of Uni Mensa Hardenbergstrasse by JOI-Design.

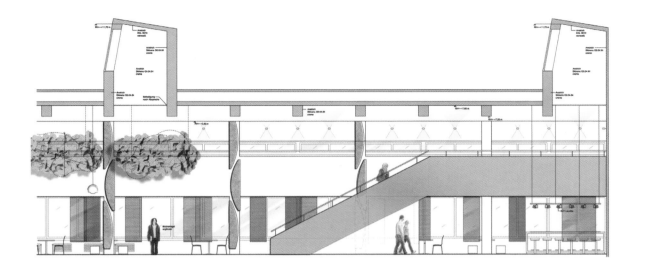

Color Plate 10
The need was to maintain a conversation-friendly environment for the large two-level space. Part of the acoustical solution includes sound absorbing art, such as leaf-shaped, felt-covered boards covering walls and columns in addition to the felt clouds. Final design presentation section elevation (computer illustration), of Uni Mensa Hardenbergstrasse by JOI-Design.

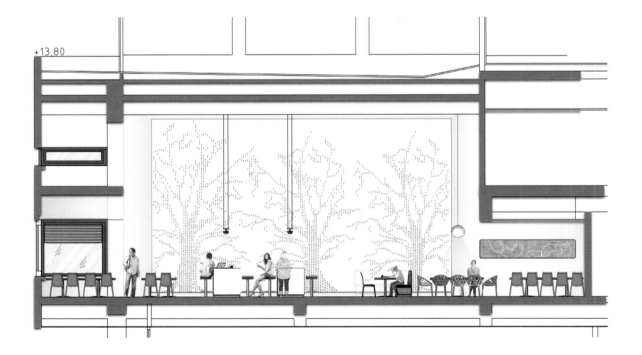

+13,80

Color Plate 11
The dominant design feature is a wall with hundreds of backlit wood blocks forming the shapes of trees rising to the upper level. Final design presentation section elevation (computer illustration) of Uni Mensa Hardenbergstrasse by JOI-Design.

Color Plate 12
Photograph of the finished project installation of Uni Mensa Hardenbergstrasse by JOI-Design.

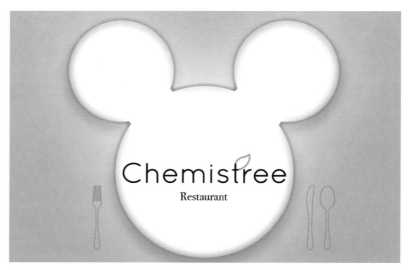

Color Plate 13
The design objective for this student project is to create a fun and interactive restaurant in Walt Disney World's Epcot Center that stimulates child education on healthy eating. (Syracuse University Senior Thesis Project, Chemistree, by Kristyn Hill. Design © Kristyn Hill.)

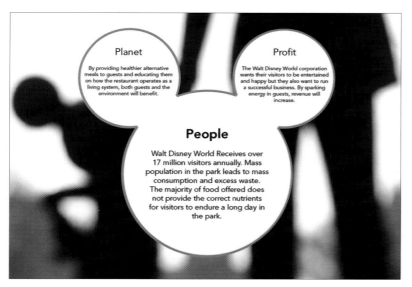

Color Plate 14
The concept is a kinetic "Mad Science Food Lab" that fuses together a biotic relationship with the visitors; the space will act as a catalyst for enjoyment in healthier eating and respect for the environment. (Syracuse University Senior Thesis Project, Chemistree, by Kristyn Hill. Design © Kristyn Hill.)

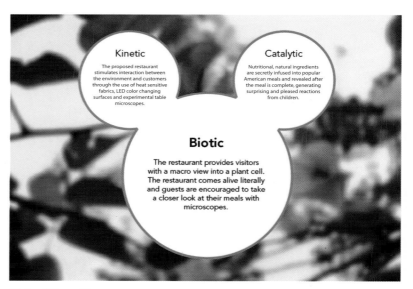

Color Plate 15
Presentation visual defining the concept. (Syracuse University Senior Thesis Project, Chemistree, by Kristyn Hill. Design © Kristyn Hill.)

Color Plate 16
Inspiration visual. (Syracuse University Senior Thesis Project, Chemistree, by Kristyn Hill. Design © Kristyn Hill.)

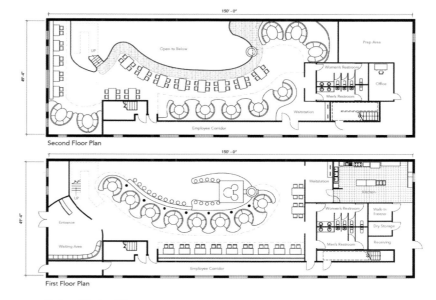

Color Plate 17
Floor plans. (Syracuse University Senior Thesis Project, Chemistree, by Kristyn Hill. Design © Kristyn Hill.)

Color Plate 18
Sitting under the microscope. Illustration showing macro images on wall and drop down magnifiers. (Syracuse University Senior Thesis Project, Chemistree, by Kristyn Hill. Design © Kristyn Hill.)

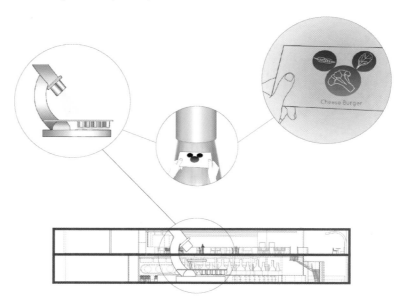

Color Plate 19
Section elevation and details. (Syracuse University Senior Thesis Project, Chemistree, by Kristyn Hill. Design © Kristyn Hill.)

Color Plate 20
Illustration depicting living walls shaped as science beakers. (Syracuse University Senior Thesis Project, Chemistree, by Kristyn Hill. Design © Kristyn Hill.)

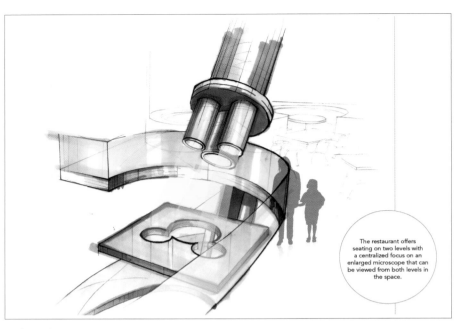

Color Plate 21
Illustration of enlarged microscope design feature. (Syracuse University Senior Thesis Project, Chemistree, by Kristyn Hill. Design © Kristyn Hill.)

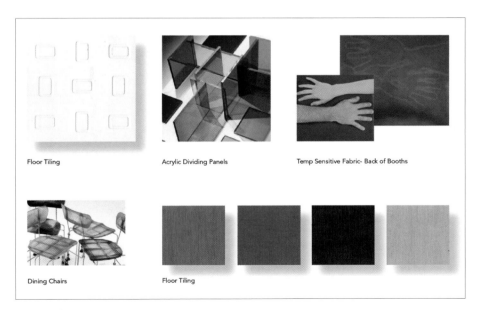

Color Plate 22
Material samples. (Syracuse University Senior Thesis Project, Chemistree, by Kristyn Hill. Design © Kristyn Hill.)

Color Plate 23
Interactive presentation using glass slides. (Syracuse University Senior Thesis Project, Chemistree, by Kristyn Hill. Design © Kristyn Hill.)

Color Plate 24
Interactive presentation viewed with magnifying glass.
(Syracuse University Senior Thesis Project, Chemistree,
by Kristyn Hill. Design © Kristyn Hill.)

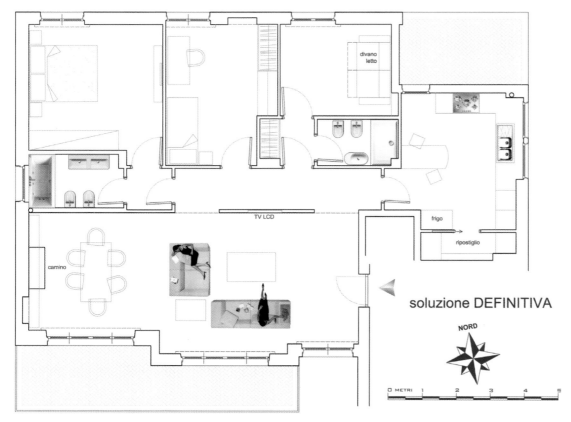

soluzione DEFINITIVA

NORD

0 METRI 1 2 3 4 5

Color Plate 25
A two-dimensional furniture plan (computer
illustration) of a residential space by Roberto
De Angelis, designed by Franco Bernardini.
Some visuals, like a furniture plan or floor
plan, could remain in view during the entire
segment. Such a visual could function as a
"you are here" map of the space, linking the
viewer to related immersive visuals, such as a
rendering or an elevation view.

Color Plate 26
A three-dimensional immersive view (computer illustration) of a residential space by Roberto De Angelis, and designed by Franco Bernardini.

Color Plate 27
3-D model of Arsoa Cosmetics visitor center by Mauk Design. (http://www .maukdesign.com/index.php#mi=2&pt=1&pi=10000&s=0&p=0&a=2&at=0)

See Chapter 9 for Color Plates 28–34

(a)

Color Plate 28
Inspiration graphics for a hotel bedroom suite by interior designer Garry Cohn (a). Loose-style illustration for a hotel bedroom suite (b). (The Royal Insurance Building Hotel concept, Liverpool, England.)

(b)

(a)

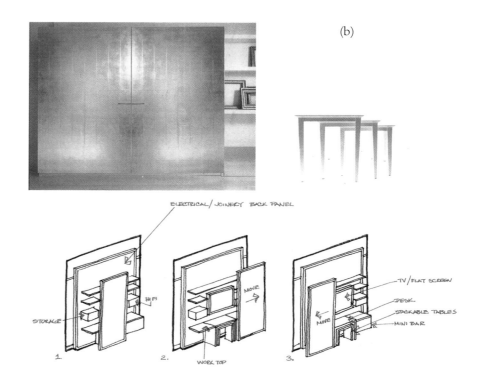

(b)

ELECTRICAL/JOINERY BACK PANEL

STORAGE

HI FI

1.

WORK TOP

2.

MOVE

MOVE

TV/FLAT SCREEN

DESK

STACKABLE TABLES

MINI BAR

3.

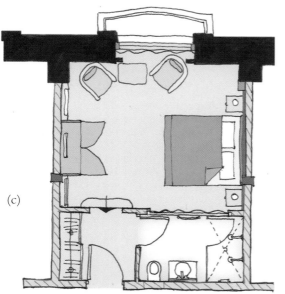

(c)

Color Plate 29
Loose-style illustration for a hotel living area suite by interior designer Garry Cohn (a). Inspiration graphics and loose-style detail illustration for a hotel suite storage wall (b). Freehand-style floor plan for a hotel suite concept (c). (The Royal Insurance Building Hotel concept, Liverpool, England.)

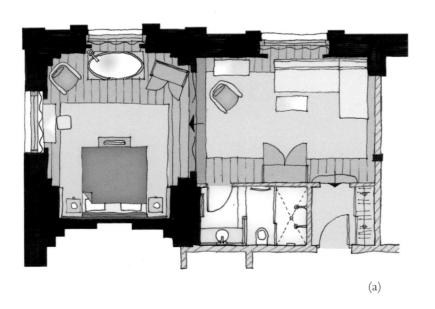

(a)

(c)

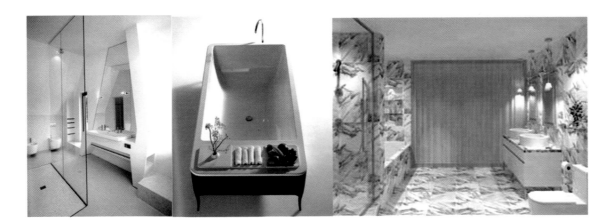

(b)

Color Plate 30
Freehand-style floor plan for a hotel deluxe suite concept by interior designer Garry Cohn (a). Inspiration graphics for a hotel deluxe suite (b). Freehand-style illustration for a hotel deluxe suite living area (c). Freehand-style illustration for a hotel deluxe suite bedroom area concept (d). Presentation board graphics of living area furnishings for a hotel deluxe suite concept (e). Presentation board graphics of furnishings for a hotel deluxe suite concept (f). (The Royal Insurance Building Hotel concept, Liverpool, England.)

(d)

(e)

(f)

Color Plate 31

Pen and digital hybrid illustration by Art & Design Studios. Hand–computer hybrids such as this are quick to produce. Art & Design Studios can produce this work at the designer's studio to help visualize design quickly and in close collaboration with designers. (Wren's Nest Museum, lobby interior. Tabassum Zolotravala.)

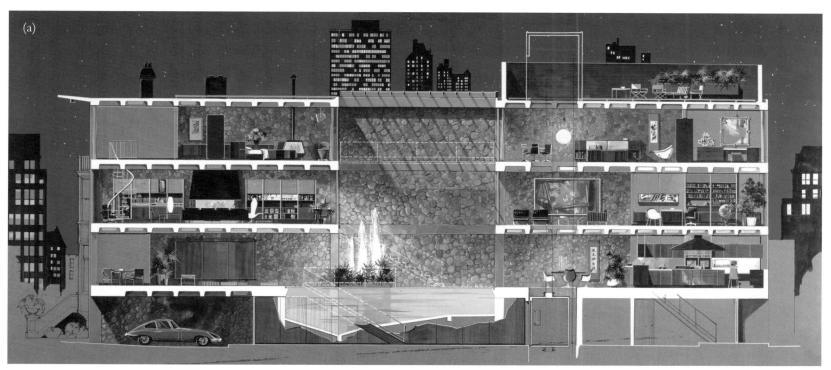

Color Plate 32
Building section elevation (a), living room (b), and dining room (c) of the Playboy Town House. Humen Tan (20th Century). Gouache and ink on illustration board. Townhouse design by architect–designer R. Donald Jaye in 1962.

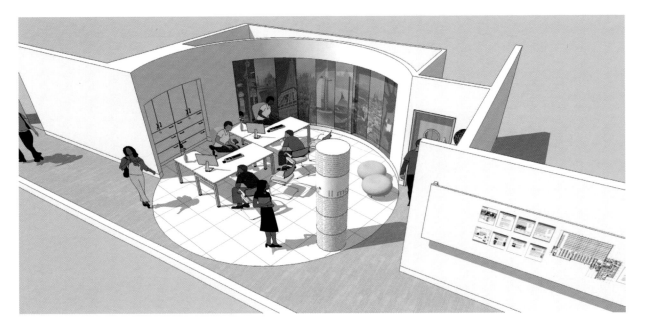

Color Plate 33
Computer illustration, cutaway view, with a bird's eye or aerial perspective viewpoint. Removing the wall and the height of the viewpoint allows the viewer to see into the space. Illustrations by pixelorchard for Mamas and Papas Travel Centre by Walton Horsfall Partnership.

Color Plate 34
People add scale and life to a rendering. The transparency of the ghost figures allows the viewer to see all of the design details. Selected 3-D model views can be exported in JPEG format and painted, softened, or given lighting effects in Photoshop. Digital Illustration by StudioDIM Associati of the Landsbanki Headquarters, Reykjavik, Iceland. Design by DAP Studio, Milan, Italy.

Idea Exchange

Media experts and graphic design professionals offer these tips to utilize in your presentation strategies:

- Typographic Hierarchy. Tony Pritchard. http://vimeo .com/13418563.
- Rory Sutherland: Life Lessons From An Ad Man. www.ted .com/talks/lang/eng/rory_sutherland_life_lessons_from_an_ ad_man.html.
- 3 Ways To Wow Your Audience With A Killer Live Presentation by Amber Mac. www.fastcompany.com/1762922/ behind-the-podium-3-tips-to-wow-your-audience-with-a-killer-presentation.

Create Experience

Design Twist Toolkits

Tell your project story. Go back to your research phase and create a wallpaper gallery mapping out the design story with notes and images.

- A timeline and relationship of people involved using Post-it Note shapes.
- Repeat the above for your presentation story.
- Use the storyboard technique and develop your presentation strategy. Print or copy file from CD.

Engage

Visit a local establishment, bank, restaurant, hotel, and retail shop. Utilize interview and doodle techniques to "tell me the story" of how you experienced the customer journey. Describe the process, draw each step of the experience (from parking the car to purchasing an item), and discuss the positive interactions.

Make an experience blueprint for one of your design projects.

Discussion and Improvisation

Read the article "10 Portfolio Commandments" by Rick Tharp at the Web site HOW, Design Ideas at Work (www. howdesign.com/article/PortfolioCommandments/).

Present the key message of one of your projects in only five minutes.

6 Performing Arts

A number of years ago I gave a presentation at a venerable Midwestern art school that still resided in its atmospheric but somewhat tired Arts & Crafts–era building. My presentation was to take place in a picturesque lecture room that apparently doubled as a life-drawing studio. My visuals were projected on a tack board wall (painted white in the distant past) pocked with pushpin holes. There was a door in the middle of the projection surface. Every slide had the door with the doorknob in the middle of the image. I hoped someone would come through the door from the next room and enter one of my portfolio images to surreal effect. Unfortunately that did not occur, although in the middle of my presentation, the school's fire alarm went off, interrupting us for about fifteen minutes while we shivered on the school's front steps. This school now enjoys its own crisp new building, having joined a university with deeper pockets.[1]

— Katherine McCoy, FIDSA

Most designers prefer to make presentations in their own conference rooms to have control over the environment and to set up the action. Luckily, we often get to travel to wonderful places and make the presentation at the client's facilities. That requires a huge amount of time in preparations and travel and, unfortunately, many things can go wrong.

Venue Considerations

The venue is your theater space. Be in command of it, and create the right tone and ambiance for the presentation. You are the set designer and the stage director now. Visualize how you will be presenting for a few moments. Design presentations typically are to small groups, and the room size and arrangement must allow eye contact with the visuals and the presenter. This strategy builds community, collaboration, and teamwork. Think about how much flexibility, connectivity, and collaboration are appropriate for the presentation and available in the meeting space.

Physical properties and equipment must support the presentation. Does it accommodate display of the various media you use to deliver your presentation? Is there a proper line of sight for your media type, and will it accommodate the attendees? Other key items to consider early are the lighting, acoustics, air circulation and temperature, power, technology and equipment needs, and hospitality activities and courtesies. Be certain to take a tour of the room ahead of time to consider its efficiency concerning all of the functional requirements when you are presenting in unfamiliar spaces. Do whatever you can to become comfortable with the presentation space.

Venues for Students

Students should have the opportunity to present in a professional setting for important milestones such as a final studio project presentation. This is necessary for senior-level students in studio or professional practice-related course work. If this is not possible, consider these options:

- Set up the classroom into arrangements similar to those in Figures 6.1 through 6.3.
- Arrange to use a campus conference room or one in a local public library.
- Arrange to present at a design office after work hours.

If your student presentation occurs in a classroom, minimize distractions by setting up single chairs for the viewers in front of you. If possible, you should be located on the wall opposite the classroom entry door to minimize disruption from persons entering or leaving the room. All viewers must focus their attention on the person presenting, not on items on their desks or their own project. The other presenters deserve this courtesy. Don't rain on their parades, and expect them not to rain on yours.

Small multipurpose spaces such as a conference room, training room, or classroom fulfill similar needs for presentations. They must:

- Support presentation attendees, documents, and media
- Provide connectivity with access to power, data, and wired and wireless device connections
- Promote communication in real time, and perhaps record dialogue or recall material presented
- Accommodate a variety of activities

▶ If you arrive late for another student's presentation and are permitted to enter, leave your belongings outside the room, enter softly, and take the seat nearest the door. Do not barge in. You can retrieve your belongings at break time.

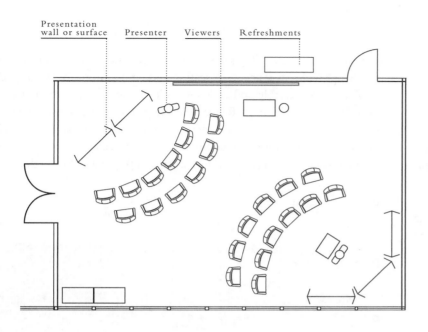

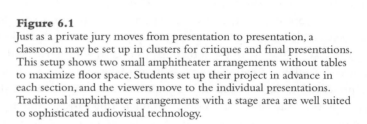

Presentation wall or surface   Presenter   Viewers   Refreshments

Figure 6.1
Just as a private jury moves from presentation to presentation, a classroom may be set up in clusters for critiques and final presentations. This setup shows two small amphitheater arrangements without tables to maximize floor space. Students set up their project in advance in each section, and the viewers move to the individual presentations. Traditional amphitheater arrangements with a stage area are well suited to sophisticated audiovisual technology.

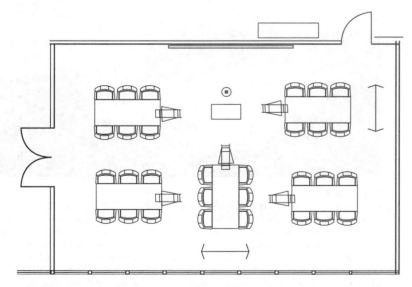

Figure 6.2
The same space may be set up for five individual presentations for smaller viewing groups, including a table for note taking. This arrangement is also called team meeting, or clusters, and is often used for group problem-solving sessions.

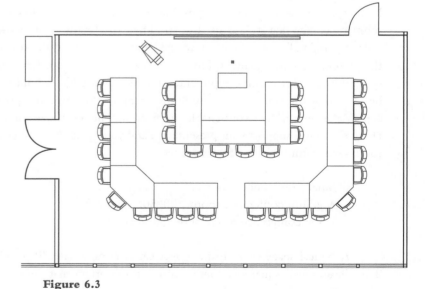

Figure 6.3
This arrangement style is a classroom or lecture presentation setup with a U-shape table configuration. The U-shape improves the line of sight to the presenter for every viewer and encourages dialogue. The configuration is used for speaking engagements, teaching, and training seminars.

Technology and Equipment

Environment has a substantial effect on performance. A small, one-person company definitely favors having the presentation in its own office. It is more practical to set up the presentation and may be done the day before the presentation. Sophisticated technology and equipment do not always work exactly the way we expect. Often, the host company has a dedicated staff available to assist in setup procedures. In that case, be sure to make contact with the individual to discuss your needs, and arrange to have them attend your presentation. Make arrangements before the presentation date for required equipment and setup, and test that equipment the day before, if possible. Do the testing early on the day of the presentation, at the latest. Get used to the equipment, learn how to use it, and make sure it works correctly. Request the name and number of whom to contact if there are problems. You may also provide your own equipment to be on the safe side.

Configurations

Many types of arrangements are possible, but generally a formal boardroom or conference style is used or modified to classroom or lecture style. Again, in all cases, the entry to the room should be at the rear of the presentation arrangement. This allows people to enter or leave the space without disrupting the presenter. Refreshment tables would also be located at the rear or just outside the entrance door in a reception area. Make certain the layout enables interaction. The room size and arrangement must support your presentation and your goals. A conference room ranges from 250 to 750 square feet.

- Small conference room: 250–300 square feet
- Medium conference room: 300–500 square feet
- Large conference room: 500–750 square feet

A typical space of 750 square feet can accommodate 30 people. This allows for 25 square feet per person. It is important that the layout

of the room not only allows the viewers to see the presenter and visuals but also provides easy access to seating and elbow room for the attendees. A conference table and chairs is the traditional design presentation room layout and the most formal. Conference or presentation facilities offer a few basic room setups, depending on your needs. These typical layout configurations are conference, Web-based and teleconference, presentation or lecture, theater, and classroom (Figures 6.4 though 6.12).

Presentation wall or projection screen   Presenter   Viewers   Refreshments

Figure 6.4
Conference arrangements are excellent for communication and interaction. They also provide surface area for visuals, note taking, and beverages, and ample space for visual presentations and electronic conferencing. The chairs nearest the visual presentation may be removed to allow free movement for one or two presenters at the head or side of the table. Tables are available in various shapes, such as rectangular, square, round, oval, crescent, V- or U-shaped, and, for much larger groups of 17 to 30 people, a hollow center arrangement with multiple tables.

Figure 6.5
A living room layout provides a casual and relaxed atmosphere that may be utilized for brainstorming sessions, shout-outs, game playing, writing, drawing, sharing, probing, informal meetings, visually presenting, and electronic conferencing. *(Herman Miller products Intersect Portfolio, and Celeste Seating in Education Area, Chicago NDC, NeoCon 2005)*

Figure 6.6
Conference rooms providing virtual collaboration are ideal for small-to-large groups who cannot afford the time or expense to travel for a face-to-face meeting. Presentations may actually be a combination of face-to-face and virtual meetings planned during the phases of a design project. An example is this setup of Herman Miller products, including Charles and Ray Eames table and molded plastic chairs, shown at Chicago NDC, NeoCon 2005.

Hospitality Courtesies

After the venue is determined, it is time to address attendee needs and contact the client. Don't forget to accommodate any person with special needs when setting up the venue arrangements. Double-check the number of people attending from the client contact list. If you are responsible for refreshments, make those arrangements ahead of time.

Remember, the refreshment area is set up in the area near the door, the rear of the room, or just outside the room. Provide choices of beverages and adequate quantities. While refreshments are typically light for a presentation, there are times when full lunches are served. This occurs during lengthy formal meetings or presentations when both parties prefer not to leave the venue space. Leaving the presentation venue interrupts the flow of a meeting. Celebratory dining after a presentation

Refreshments   Projection Screen Podium Presenter

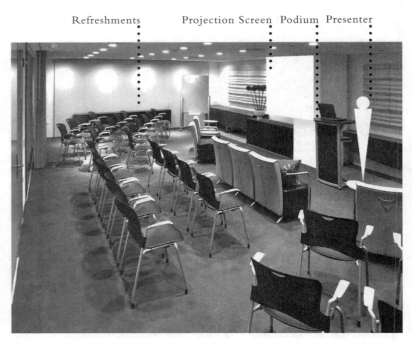

Figure 6.7
An informal setting for small groups with virtual conferencing capability. A circle or semicircle is ideal for small groups, and the freedom of the arrangement encourages participation. Other variations of the arrangement include the fish bowl or double circle. The chairs are arranged in two concentric circles and facing each other but widely spaced from side to side. The arrangement encourages one-on-one interaction between two people from different perspectives—one inside the fish bowl and the other on the outside of the fish bowl. *(Herman Miller products Charles and Ray Eames Soft Pad Chairs and George Nelson Bubble Lights)*

Figure 6.8
Theater- or auditorium-style configurations are used for lectures or large groups when note taking is not required. The layout has either a center aisle or side aisles or both. Each row is tiered (not shown), improving the sight line for the viewers. Seating should be removed from locations where the view of speaker or presentation is obscured by a column or other obstruction. A viewing angle of less than 30 degrees to the presentation area is too acute for ease of vision. *(Herman Miller products Celeste and Caper Chairs, Chicago NDC, NeoCon 2005)*

is common practice among designers and clients. Accommodate any special dietary needs such as vegetarian, kosher or halal, or diabetic requirements, and so on.

Determine the travel and accommodation needs a month in advance. Work out the logistics of catering, transportation, and parking more than a week in advance. Also, consider shipping presentation materials ahead of time and confirm that they have arrived.

▶ You can now begin to write a preliminary agenda for the presentation and revise it, as needed, while making all preparations. Distribute the preliminary agenda to all who need to know, so they can use it as a basis for their individual task list and preparation.

Figure 6.9
The classroom configuration of rows of narrow tables and chairs facing the presenter is desirable for long lectures and note taking but does not encourage interaction among viewers. *(Steelcase product, ēno interactive white board with a 3-in-1 combination dry erase, magnetic, and interactive whiteboard)*

Figure 6.10
Multimedia room.

At this point, revise your preliminary agenda and have a colleague look at it and the presentation. Ask him or her if you are missing anything or have included too much. Finally, after the participants and venue are determined, it is time to contact the client again. In this courtesy call, let them know who will be attending, what their background is, what their contribution to the project is, and their purpose for attending. In a friendly and succinct way, pass on all key pieces of information to the client, including the purpose of the presentation, what the presentation is about, what they will see, approximate duration and planned breaks, who will be there, and the scheduled time and place.

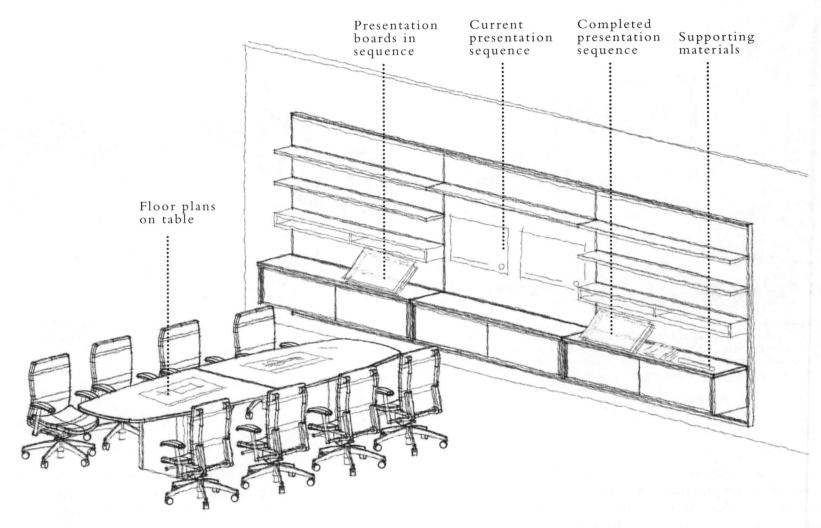

Presentation
boards in
sequence

Current
presentation
sequence

Completed
presentation
sequence

Supporting
materials

Floor plans
on table

Figure 6.11
Conference room showing table perpendicular to the presentation wall.

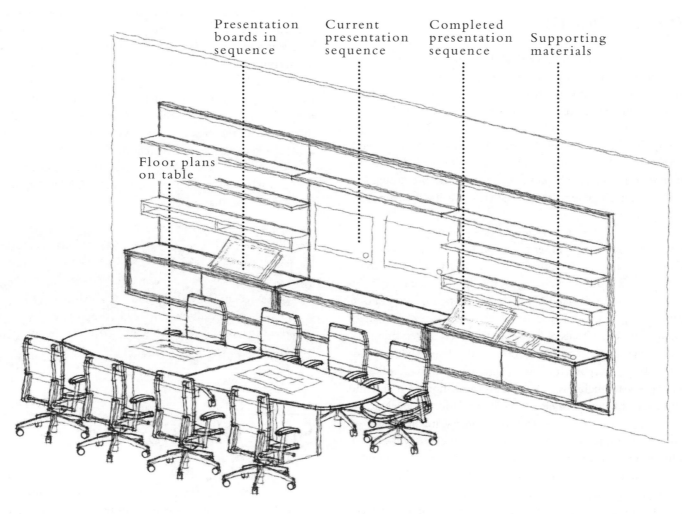

Presentation boards in sequence

Current presentation sequence

Completed presentation sequence

Supporting materials

Floor plans on table

Figure 6.12
Conference room showing table parallel to the presentation wall.

Survey the Scene

Details matter. Spend enough time checking the presentation environment and eliminate anything that is distracting. You want to immerse the client in the design event you have carefully prepared, not an untidy space. All presentation white boards should be clean. Your coat, briefcase, portfolio case, handbag, and the like are visual clutter. Find a place to store them out of sight. Remove unnecessary items from the conference table and arrange the chairs neatly. Remove chairs if they will be in the way of your presenting space. The conference table and presenting surfaces should be clean. In general, remove anything from the room that will be a visual distraction.

Sit in the seats of the viewers to check sightlines and eliminate obstructions. Plan where you will set up the visuals. Put yourself in the position of the viewers and determine whether they will be able to see the visuals clearly and hear you well. Adjust the lighting, windows, window coverings, and doors as needed for the presentation. They should aid visibility, hearing, and comfort for the viewers. Organize and check all requirements for your visuals to make sure you have everything you need and that everything is in proper working order. Easels, whiteboards, drawing and writing pads, pens, tracing roll and markers, architect's scale, tack pins and tape, leave-behinds, and business cards should be on hand. Be sure to have backup copies of electronic presentations. Check power and equipment to ensure they are working properly, including laptop, computer, projector, projection surfaces, remote control device, pointers, microphone, and power cords. Test every one of them. Neutralize all electronic distractions, such as electric and computer cords, lens caps, equipment carrying cases, and the like.

What you can have in the room are the items that support and enhance the presentation. Countless ways to create a positive visual and functional connection experience are possible. Find ways to engage the senses with cues related to the project or design concept in some way. It all adds to an enhanced experience for the attendees. You are a designer and can be as creative and unique as you like. After all, you are planning an event and can make it a memorable experience. Stationary portfolio, writing pads, pencils, water pitchers, coffee urns, and glassware are necessary. The next level could include arrangements of fresh flowers, fruit bowls, or small edible items such as candies, mints, or nuts. These items are not part of the refreshments. Do not allow the placement to interfere with the presentation or viewing space. Music or aroma, when well related to the design concept or client tastes, adds even more drama. These can be successful mood enhancements, but be thoughtful about allergies while determining those extras. Clients are special people, so make them feel that way.

> ▶ "I'm not interested in the product itself—that's not what is important. It is how it makes people feel. I want to connect as many people as possible. They all react differently to a piece like the Knotted Chair. Some just want to touch it. Some will want to know exactly how it was made—they just want to tell how beautiful they think it is. This is how different people read life. I've got to communicate with all of them." Marcel Wanders

Stage Direction

Jonathan McClellan offers an important acting tip to apply to your presentation technique. He says, "Remember that you are showing a story, not telling it. Everything you do must work to show the audience the story." This includes your entire personality: breath, movements, and words. When you are relaxed, free and spontaneous, your real personality presents itself. That is what the viewer wants to see. You can benefit from basic acting training to learn how to hold your body for best posture and voice control, projection, enunciation, and breathing. When you speak clearly and with confidence, you help define your position as an expert on your topics. The Alexander Technique teaches how to retrain bad physical habits and how to develop efficient breathing, vocalization, gesture, movement, poise, and grace. Remember this: You learn design by experience, and likewise, you learn presentation skills by experience. The acting profession offers these tips:

Warm Up Your Body

When you are nervous or stressed, the feeling will create tension in many parts of your body. Perform stretching exercises or yoga before going into a presentation to help you get the blood flowing, relax, and reduce the stress you may be feeling. Simple relaxation exercises used by actors and dancers to prepare their body before going on stage are shaking, bobbing, swaying, and circling.

> ▶ "My musical training found me lying on the floor many times to practice breathing techniques and performing exercises in proper diction. Obviously, none of that found its way into my design education; yet neither did any rigorous instruction on the fundamentals of preparing a concise verbal argument." Andrew Caruso, Gensler

Warm Up Your Voice

The late movie actress Bette Davis walked around her home holding a wine cork loosely between her front teeth to keep her jaw loose. A few thespian tips for keeping your voice warmed up can work for you as well. Drink warm water because cold water restricts vocal cords. Sip hot water with lemon before the presentation and during breaks. Keep the volume of your voice at a normal level for a natural performance.

Change the volume of your voice or microphone if the audience asks you to do so. The tiny lavaliere microphones are tucked under a collar or lapel. Be sure that the tip of the microphone peeks out a bit but that the microphone tip is not touching any clothing. Remember to hide the wire in clothing.

> ▶ Most people do not like the sound of their own voice. Rather than uttering "um" or "err," pause and look at your viewers.

Find Your Light

You will have general illumination in the room and spot lighting on you and the presentation. In stage acting, the actors find their light by feeling it in their face and eyes. The actual light projected is at an angle toward your forehead. Never stand directly under hot spots because you will look washed out from glare. If the only light is from below your face, you will look ghoulish from shadows on your face. If there is not enough light on you, you will appear gloomy. The best way to light a speaker who is standing in a fixed position, such as a podium, is with three lights. The key light is at the left side and above the speaker, directed toward the speaker; a softer backlight is positioned behind the speaker, above and to the side; and the fill light is positioned to the right side, mid-level of the speaker.

Stay Open

Stay open, both mentally and physically. Be aware of your body position at all times. Presenters, like actors, always face forward or angle their body toward the audience. Never turn your back toward the viewers. When directing the viewer to a visual, stand to the side of the visual, facing out, and gesture to the visual with your arm or a pointing device.

> ▶ Do not talk to the visuals—talk to the viewers.

Move

Never deliver a presentation while seated. It is acceptable for an informal design process, or in-house meeting, but not for a formal presentation. Likewise, do not stand in the exact same spot during the presentation. You can move around and play the room in a natural way to connect with the viewers. Position yourself close to the visuals and the viewers. Do not stand between a projector and the screen. Focus your mind on the design you are selling, but focus your eyes on the viewers. Do not leave a visual in place if it is no longer relevant to the discussion. Likewise, do not leave projection equipment on if the screen is a blank white light. Place your pointing device on the table or presentation ledge when you are not using it. Use your body to quietly help viewers recognize transitions by a change in your voice or gestures. The audience will look at you when you move, and it is a way to focus their attention. Remember, no slouching, leaning, swaying or rocking in place, or pacing.

The task for you, as the designer, is to create a meaningful interaction with your viewers in order to persuade them to accept your design solution. A boring delivery is one that is overly professorial and rigid. If that is the case, no matter how talented you are or how great the idea is, the viewers will not warm up to you. Likewise, if the delivery is overly casual in attitude you run a risk of not being taken seriously.

> ▶ "An effective speaker displays energy, empathy, enthusiasm, engagement, and entertainment when delivering presentations." David Greusel, AIA

Overcoming Stage Fright

Fear is often the way we express our lack of confidence. Sometimes fear is a form of procrastination. Fear will definitely interfere with your ability to get where you want to go. Look at it this way: Personal benefits result from a successful presentation. By shifting your thinking to what you can achieve instead of your fears, you will be triumphant. Quite simply, a delighted client equals success, and that leads to additional work, career advancement, and financial benefits. Now, warm up to those thoughts. You may say, "But even that makes me nervous, with so much at stake." I say, "Get out of your way—use this to push you forward." Give your viewer your confidence in yourself and the project because it will help them to trust your solutions. The project is the center of attention and your job is to help the viewer focus on it. Ask yourself these two questions: What could happen? What is most likely to happen?

In many ways, a preliminary presentation is more risky than a final presentation. During that phase, you are presenting and testing new ideas that the client has not seen yet. Clients have faith in you, and that is why they hired you. Have faith in your presentation, happiness about your solutions, and confidence that they will like it. It's the honeymoon phase. It will build a stronger and deeper relationship with the client. Relax, knowing that it is the most likely thing that will happen and the most valuable benefit.

Finally, remember that you are on the verge of giving an idea its reality. Breathe life into it with enthusiasm. This point in a project gives clients a vision of their future and something tangible to pin their hopes on. The next phases of a project, construction documents, bidding, and the actual building process, may take a long time to complete, and enthusiasm can wane. The presentation is something that you and the client can use later to renew and reaffirm your joint commitment to a better world. They all want to see and hear what you have to say, so enjoy yourself and be enthusiastic about presenting your solutions to them. Remember that the end user is the center of the story. Put people first.

To facilitate this process, it is important that you obtain feedback from your practice sessions. Then you will know your weaknesses and can develop a plan to prevail over them. You can overcome your fears this way:

- Believe in your solutions.
- Be well prepared. Leave nothing to chance. Know what you are going to say. Know your audience. Know the conditions.
- Practice. Practice again.
- Have a backup.
- Arrive at the presentation early enough to set up, perform a final check, and chat with the attendees as they arrive.
- View the audience as friends, or pretend you are alone.
- Don't look at a person whose expression bothers you.
- Project a positive image. Think of yourself as having something very important to say. You do.
- Relax before you speak by taking a few very deep breaths.
- Count to ten before starting. This allows the viewers time to settle themselves.

> "Gain self-confidence and speak loud and clearly. Don't look back to the screen when you do the presentation; look into the faces of the audience." Peter Joehnk, principal at JOI-Design

You can also prepare yourself to recover from slipups this way:

- Your mind goes blank
  ‣ Find a trigger point in your visual.
  ‣ Refer to your outline notes.
  ‣ Select a person to focus your eyes on for a few seconds, then another until you are back on track.

‣ Smile and take a deep breath.
‣ Repeat what you had just said or ad-lib something similar to trigger your mind.
‣ Ask someone a question such as, "What are your thoughts so far, Ruth?"
‣ Say, "Where was I?"
- Trembling
  ‣ Eliminate caffeine beforehand and drink water or juice.
  ‣ Accept your nervousness and direct it to enthusiasm.
  ‣ Picture yourself with confidence and authority.
  ‣ Move a bit and use body gestures while speaking.
  ‣ Massage your forehead.
  ‣ Breathe deeply.
  ‣ Look at the viewers with whom you have a friendly relationship.
  ‣ Smile and take a deep breath.
  ‣ Share an anecdote from the project to break the ice.
- Voice
  ‣ Practice difficult and important words before the presentation.
  ‣ Be expressive with your voice.
  ‣ Concentrate on the positive emotions you feel about the design.
  ‣ Speak more slowly if you are a non-native speaker.
  ‣ Drink a glass of water.
  ‣ Breathe deeply with the support of your diaphragm.
  ‣ Pause at key points.

Singers and actors learn to breathe from their diaphragm because it allows them to take in more air, but it also helps you to control your speaking voice. With this method, you fill your lower lungs with air as opposed to your upper lungs when you breathe in. The result will expand your diaphragm, not your chest. Conversely, use your diaphragm to push the air out of your lungs. Other ways to improve your delivery are through professional instruction and practice. Many resources are available, including communication courses, acting and voice classes, and coaching from professional voice, acting, and public speaking experts. While you may not be making presentations every day of your life, you will be making presentations for the rest of your life as an interior designer.

> ▶ Complete the setup before anyone arrives for the meeting. Use the time immediately proceeding to greet and mingle with attendees. Project your friendliness and then perform.

Perform

Get into character for the presentation. Take your place. *Energy, Eye Contact,* and *Expression.* Be silent for a moment to allow everyone to focus his or her attention on the presentation. Show everyone how happy and excited you are about the project by smiling. Naturally, you should be yourself, authentic, relaxed, and sincere. Nonetheless, you must also be completely prepared for the presentation. Don't forget that you are the specialist today and know the most about what you are presenting. Most designers begin with a brief review of what will be presented, the general project, and the process taken to solve the design to help orient the client to their methods. If you find yourself in an unfortunate situation, such as Katherine McCoy did, take it in stride. Make the most of it by arranging to walk through that door to make a surrealistic presentation entrance. Then improvise by tacking large sheets of white paper to the surface or present with the printed back-up materials.

> ▶ Do have a set of plans, a roll of tissue, colored drawing pencils or markers on the table. Events will occur where you may need to draw alternatives in response to objections. In addition, designers have clients sign off on a plan after a presentation is complete.

Dialogue with Peter Joehnk

JOI-Design, Hamburg, Germany
Peter Joehnk and Corinna Kretschmar-Joehnk, Principals

Q. What is your preferred venue for making design presentations to a client?

A. Clearly our office!

Q. What is your setup procedure? How many people from your office usually attend a design presentation? What do their tasks include?

A. Unpack our boards and connect my laptop with the beamer (projector), if we are in the client's office. If we do the presentation in our office, we also care for drinks and snacks. Maximum is three people; sometimes I do it alone. Tasks are to take notes and to present the mood board with the original materials while I am doing the digital presentation.

Q. Do you have an agenda to keep to once a presentation begins?

A. Yes, the format of the presentation with the beamer requires to stay "in line"—but I am happy to answer questions and jump back sometimes.[2]

Idea Exchange

- First read the transcript, and then watch and be inspired by "Natasha Tsakos' Multimedia Theatrical Adventure." The timing of her gestures is exquisite. www.ted.com/talks/ natasha_tsakos_multimedia_theatrical_adventure.html.

Create Experience

Acting

Practice saying the following phrases with feeling:

The high ceilings and columns of the restored interior are a cool white; the hardwood flooring is stained a deep ebony to set off the furniture's sculptural lines. Subtle, sophisticated track lighting further emphasizes each piece.[3]

Practice saying the phrases with a pause at the | | symbols:

The high ceilings | | and columns of the restored interior are a cool white; the hardwood flooring is stained | | a deep ebony | | to set off the furniture's sculptural lines. | | Subtle, sophisticated track lighting further emphasizes each piece.

Practice saying the phrases with emphasis on the words in **bold** type:

The **high** ceilings and columns of the restored interior are a **cool** white; the hardwood flooring is stained a **deep** ebony to set off the **furniture's** sculptural lines. **Subtle, sophisticated** track lighting further emphasizes each piece.

Practice saying the phrases with eye contact, body movements, hand gestures, and a design visual such as a plan, illustration, or color and material board:

The high ceilings and columns of the restored interior are a cool white; the hardwood flooring is stained a deep ebony to set off the furniture's sculptural lines. Subtle, sophisticated track lighting further emphasizes each piece.

Repeat the exercise while video-recording yourself, and play back the recording.

Improvisation

This exercise will help you to think on your feet and gain confidence in any setting. The basic premise of improv is to move the scene forward by acknowledging what was previously said, adding additional dialogue to what was said, trusting your instinct relative to what to say, and supporting other team members. All this is done at a rather quick pace, and that means no "um's" or "err's". The spirit of this exercise is acting out ideas.

Part One. Set up your stage as a presentation venue. Select three teams of presenters and three teams of audience members. Your instructor will select a completed student design project that has presentation documents for each phase of the design project: Programming, Preliminary Design, and Final Design.

Part Two. Set up each phase of the project for the presentation. You will now improvise the presentation of each phase by Presenter Team and audience members. Present and explore the design using improvisation in which all actors participate. Freely use your imagination while responding to what is distinctive to the moment.

7
Collaboration

I once had (designed) a terrazzo floor with these cobalt blue and green glass chips in the terrazzo floor. And the Japanese contractor looked at me and said, "What [sic] you talking about—glass chips? Na! No such thing!" I said, "Oh, watch me! Go get me a bottle of Coca-Cola." I cracked the bottle, "Here is your green glass. Here, put it in." Well, the next thing you know, the whole job site is drinking Coca-Cola.[1]

— Tony Chi, designer

The serendipity of the moment solved the difficulty of the floor installation and is an example of one energizing feature of successful collaboration. When designers, artists, contractors, and owners recognize happenstance and possess the skills, they are able to transform a difficulty with spontaneous collaboration. This is exemplary of how designers collaborate. Think of the green glass chips the next time you need to see a fix for opposition to your design concept.

Managing Questions and Responses

Equate is the collaboration opportunity in your presentation. This segment is when you take questions and obtain the client's consent to proceed. When you thoroughly know your viewers, you also know who is a supporter, who is neutral, and who may oppose. You also understand their biases and reservations. Make it your mission to neutralize objections with appropriate and knowledgeable replies. For work to continue collectively through the *Equate* segment, the skills of listening, respecting, participating, and deciding are indispensable. These are the same skills utilized within a design team to reach this point in the design process. According to Jay L. Brand, cognitive psychologist, "The world of work, currently involving three generations, may be shifting from primarily individual to more collaborative activities."[2]

- Listening requires that you are attentive and aim to understand what others are saying or asking. Do not be distracted by your own rationales while listening.
- Respecting is the acknowledgment of the ideas or opinions of others. Show consideration for their concerns and try to con-

nect with those concerns. Once respect is achieved, you can better explain how you have addressed or can resolve an issue.
- Participating includes contributing, sharing learned experiences, helping others, and asking questions if you do not understand a question or idea.
- Deciding is your ability to bring the group to a consensus on any issue and proceeding with a course of action.

> ► "I think the business has changed in that there is a lot of attention paid to value. People really want to make sure they are spending their money wisely, so more time is spent making decisions than in the past. Before things slowed down it was, 'How fast can you do this?' We're good at handling that, and we know how to do it, but now people take more time to make those decisions." Victoria Hagan, interior designer

> ► "Everyone is a resource. Listen carefully, even when it might seem like a distraction. Good ideas are everywhere and sometimes (a lot of times!) they come from unexpected places." Colin Brice, Mapos, LLC

Strategies and skills in this chapter for working collectively and collaboratively are relevant to each phase of the design process, applicable to both informal and formal interior design presentations and meetings, and useful for class critiques. During the *Equate* segment remain positive, do not become argumentative, and look for common ground. Design is a "social activity," according to Paula Scher, design partner of Pentagram, and it "involves other people, their opinions, comments, egos, conceits, jealousies, and fears."[3] Her advice is this: when clients have been involved with the design process, "they are often much better behaved clients. They have a basis for making visual judgments that has been depersonalized and has become more objective."[4] To be successful requires a considerable ability to harmonize with others and express empathy. You can express empathy by acknowledging that you understand how the individual feels, how others felt (use the opinions of your allies), and how you feel about a challenging issue. The empathy must be sincere and requires listening carefully to what is said. After this, you will be able to address the concerns with explanations and solutions. It is courteous to then follow up with a question such as, "Has this solved your concern?" If it hasn't, then perhaps you have not understood the concerns well enough or there is a more serious issue.

Moreover, your knowledge of the client is the most useful tool in helping formulate answers to questions and objections. If you thoroughly understand the question or objection, you next quickly consider the best way to appeal to the individual. Analyze whether a logical, ethical, or emotional appeal is the appropriate response. Some cases occur when a combination of these factors is best. Figure 7.1 shows the process of shaping a response. Massimo Vignelli considers a designer the doctor and the client the patient. He says it is our job to give them what they need, not what they want.[5] Clients may need reassurance because they are not comfortable with new ideas, they may need more facts or additional reasons that tie into the brand or identity, or they may need more faith in the solution. Architect Annabelle Selldorf was asked "What is the most important thing you have learned?" She replied, "Listening and collaborating—all the while pursuing my own path—and making use of other people's points of view. The more you know what a client wants, the more interesting it gets."[6]

> ▶ "The world is about people—not objects." Arik Levy, designer

> ▶ "Be sure to present the entire job; providing a note pad and pens for questions will keep the client quiet. When you are on stage, you do not want to hear any 'boos' or comments; everyone is quiet. Finish your presentation and then deal with the questions. Don't let them rain on your parade." Vicente Wolf, Vicente Wolf Associates

Do not try to solve a real problem in the meeting. Stay open to the feedback you are receiving. Tim Brown tells us that insight, observation, and empathy are part of a successful design program; they are also valuable skills for collaboration. It is best to write down everything discussed and say, "I will address this with further study and get back to you with a solution." That way you are not forced to come up with an alternative that may not work. Give yourself time to reflect. Personal preferences are powerful. Nevertheless, a clear difference exists between a client being unsure of new ideas and an idea that does not work. Admit when it is time to go back to the drawing board. Do remind clients of what was accomplished and help them to remain centered on the primary goals.

In general, the preference is for allowing time for questions after the presentation is complete. This is your presentation, and you are responsible for maintaining coherency and information sequence. Distractions do happen. A question may come up that would be answered in another part of the presentation. Simply say, "I will get to that in a minute." Interruptions occur in the form of a doubt. If you can quickly clarify an ambiguity, do it. At times, you may have to help someone formulate his or her own question by asking him or her to rephrase the question. Additionally, asking someone to rephrase a question allows you more time to think about and formulate an answer.

Do not interrupt anyone in the middle of his or her question. Make good eye contact. Take the question seriously. Pause and reflect before answering questions. You may restate a question (especially important

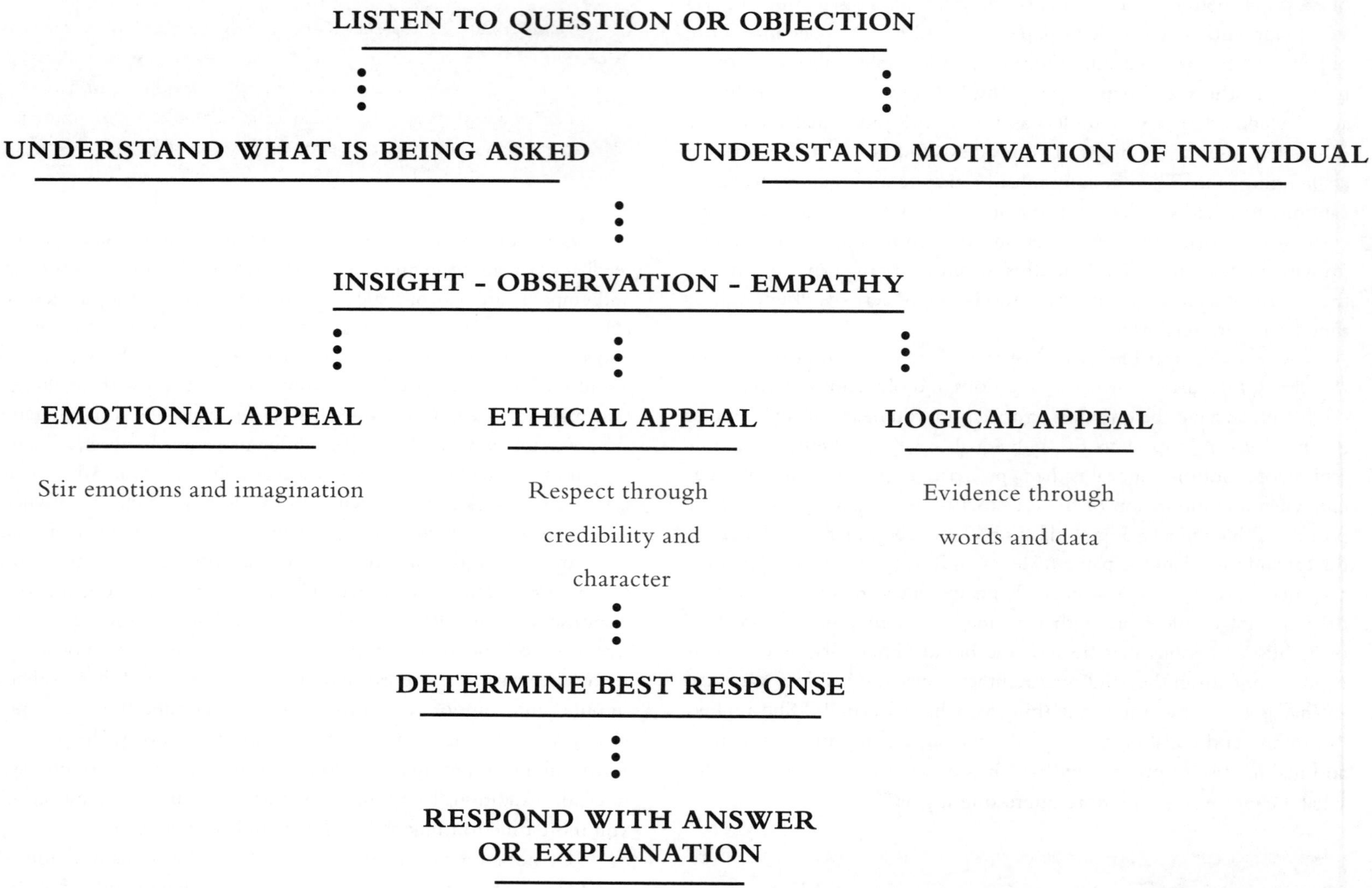

LISTEN TO QUESTION OR OBJECTION
——————————————————

UNDERSTAND WHAT IS BEING ASKED   UNDERSTAND MOTIVATION OF INDIVIDUAL
——————————————————   ——————————————————

INSIGHT – OBSERVATION – EMPATHY
——————————————————

EMOTIONAL APPEAL   **ETHICAL APPEAL**   **LOGICAL APPEAL**
————————   ————————   ————————

Stir emotions and imagination   Respect through   Evidence through

                                 credibility and   words and data

                                 character

DETERMINE BEST RESPONSE
——————————————————

RESPOND WITH ANSWER
OR EXPLANATION
——————————————————

Figure 7.1
Response method.

for large audiences) and give yourself more time to understand it and form your answer. Ask for clarification if you do not understand what is being asked. There will be times when you do not have an answer. In that case, field the question to another team member or simply say, "I will check into it and get back to you with an answer."

Managing or Framing Objections

Changes have consequences. You may need to go back and explain how you reached a decision when there is opposition. This will be easy for you if you have a thorough understanding of the options explored during the development of the project design. Your response can be, "Yes, we considered that idea also. We think this is the better solution for you because [explain the pros and cons]. . . ." If that is not sufficient, then handle the issue by taking it through a similar, but longer explanation. Take the client from one idea to the next idea and explain the consequence of each idea. Once someone can see a consequence of one idea, it is easy to understand the benefits of your original solution. Samuel Botero used humor to ease tension with his customers, as stated in Chapter 2: "If *I* had to be a chair—*I'd be that one*."[7] It helps relax the tension. Never use humor that potentially insults clients or their company, brand, or product; however, you can gently poke fun at yourself.

When clients make a request for a change that is not in the best interest of the project, it is your responsibility as a design professional to explain why it is not. Remind them of how you have met the project objectives. Help them to become comfortable with the design. They may need more convincing or more time. At this point you may need to help them establish priorities again by restating their objectives, criteria, and set up priorities for those criteria. Do not rush hesitant clients; instead, explain to them why and expand with examples. You are able to justify your recommendations because they have been purposeful choices.

Control the dialogue, be receptive, and remain on target. Massimo Vignelli believes it is important to "pay attention, evaluate the comments, and not say yes to changes automatically."[8] He believes that sometimes a client does have "creative input that can switch the direction" in a presentation. Vignelli responds well to a reason if it is valid—"but if there is no reason, we will explain why it is not a valid alternative."[9]

▶ "How do you react when a client says, 'This is not working'? By asking, 'why?' " Massimo Vignelli, Vignelli Associates

Responding to Issues of Ethics

Never agree to a change that is detrimental to the life and safety of the occupants in any facility. You should refuse to consent to or participate in any action of that type. Designers must comply with code and regulatory requirements, which are enforced by law. Moreover, it is in the best interest of the client and the designer to refrain from complying with a request that falls out of the designer's expertise. If you cannot perform the work requested, you cannot assume any responsibility to do it.

What can you do if the client says, "XXX design firm suggested that we do XXX." If you agreed to have another designer's participation, then you would respectfully consider the suggestion. If a situation occurs that interferes with or has a business consequence, tactfully explain that it may be a conflict of interest (or whatever the particular case may be). Professional designers honor a code of ethics. Your client might not know this. The American Society of Interior Designers (ASID), International Interior Design Association (IIDA), Industrial Designers Society of America (IDSA), American Institute of Architects (AIA), and Interior Designers of Canada (IDC) have clear guidelines to follow that apply to this type of situation. ASID, Code of Ethics, Section 4.0, "Responsibility to Other Interior Designers and Colleagues" states the following:[10]

4.1 Members shall not interfere with the performance of another interior designer's contractual or professional relationship with a client.

4.2 Members shall not initiate, or participate in, any discussion or activity which might result in an unjust injury to another interior designer's reputation or business relationships.

4.3 Members may, when requested and it does not present a conflict of interest, render a second opinion to a client or serve as an expert witness in a judicial or arbitration proceeding.

Explaining Design Solutions

Comments from invisible viewers do not have to upset the direction of the project. In this case, you can deflect those comments by saying, "They do not have an understanding of your project goals," or "we have done what is best for you." If the client considers their suggestions to be very valuable, you can ask the client if they want to set up a meeting with them to review the project. That way you have an opportunity to bring them around to supporting your design strategy for the project. Do this with a new key client employee, VIP, or stakeholder.

Anticipating objections and planning strategies for dealing with them is the best way to help manage this segment of a presentation. Do this bit of role-playing before the presentation. The following are some typical pet peeves of designers and ways to respond:

Request: Make this look more like XXX company (usually a competitor).

Reply: We have designed a solution unique for you to meet your requirements.

Request: James developed a great idea for this.

Reply: Sure, we can meet to review it. Let's talk about how much additional time it will require and how it will affect the project schedule, budget, and design fees.

Request: Can we change the yellow to gray?

Reply #1: We do not think it connects with your company brand (customer). (Explain why.)

Reply #2: Yes, yellow is a surprising (or powerful) choice. It definitely says that you are unique and original.

Reply #3: If we did, it would result in losing color balance (harmony, contrast, etc.).

Comment: I do not like it. It is too different. I don't know about this.

Reply #1: Why?

Reply #2: I'm sorry, let me put it another way. Yes, it *is* special (instead of different) and will express to others your position as a leader in the industry.

Your goal is to obtain approval, so if you can, solve the issue on the spot. That may require that you take the roll of tissue and draw the new suggestion to show that what was originally presented is better. Pull out the earlier concept studies to show that it was already tried and did not solve all the issues. Remember that you may also enlist your allies and team members to respond to questions that you may not be able to answer as well as they can. Do not let little details become more important than the whole.

Agreement to Proceed

Scott Simpson, FAIA warns,

> You'll never arrive at a conclusion unless the audience says "yes." Make this easy on them by having all the relevant and required information at hand—"decision-ready information"—then don't be afraid to ask for an answer. If the client can't commit, find out why. Remember that the largest part of being a good communicator is being a good listener.[11]

You do want the viewers to feel good about giving you authorization to proceed. Tim Brown says it quite well: "It's not about 'us versus them' or even 'us on behalf of them.' . . . it has to be 'us *with* them.' "[12] You also have to continue on target and discuss the next course of action. Remind the client of what is approved, what may change, and what cannot change without extra costs. Ask the client to formally sign off on the plans and documents reviewed. These documents are a mutual commitment for both the client and you. The meeting notes, which are equally important, are discussed in Chapter 8.

The client may ask for a couple of days to consider. Say, "When is the soonest date we can get your approval to proceed?" Go on to explain the implementation schedule deadlines and how important it is to meet deadlines for reasons of construction schedule and budget.

You must document everything said during the presentation. That requires good note taking. The documentation is proof of what is approved and what follow-up is needed. These follow-up items are addressed before proceeding to the next presentation or construction documents.

Congratulations on arriving at *authorization to proceed*. Share that happiness with your client and your staff. All will be feeling great pride in what you have and will accomplish together. Shake hands, thank the client, let them know you will be in contact again soon, and thank your staff. In some cultures, gift giving (or gift exchange) is very common among business professionals and may occur at this point in a presentation meeting, depending on custom. Make it your goal to end this segment with everyone feeling energized and exhilarated.

Dialogue with Peter Joehnk

JOI-Design, Hamburg, Germany
Peter Joehnk, and Corinna Kretschmar-Joehnk, Principals

Q. Do you find it difficult if, once in the final design presentation, it goes down a different path and you realize that it will have to be redesigned?

A. Yes, these are the "shit days"!

Q. What tips can you provide to handle these situations?

A. When you recognize that the design is absolutely not what the client wants, you should still be accepted as designer and respond to the situation—which can mean disagreeing with or accepting the different design strategy and coming up with a new proposal. The only thing that should not happen is that the client does not trust your competence anymore.

Q. How do you deal with a challenging client in a presentation?

A. Usually, I try to interact and to please him, but I have situations also where the "chemistry" with the client and me did not work and then—that is it.

Q. Has a client ever told you your idea was too eccentric? How did you deal with it? How do you react when a client says, "This is not working"?

A. Both reactions are standard. But clients usually want to see something that is a bit too eccentric (it is easier to step back than be eccentric later). "It does not work" is a weak argument. You know as well as the client what works and what doesn't and which compromises you have to accept.[13]

Idea Exchange

- Watch the video "Simon Sinek: How Great Leaders Inspire Action." Sinek explains a simple model for leadership, starting with the question "Why." www.ted.com/talks/simon_sinek_how_great_leaders_inspire_action.html.
- Watch the video about design and emotions, "Don Norman on 3 Ways Good Design Makes You Happy." www.ted.com/talks/lang/eng/don_norman_on_design_and_emotion.html.

Create Experience

Debate. In this exercise, the group debates a design issue as practice in developing skills of negotiation, flexibility, and support. It also affords members an opportunity to present their unique perspective on interior design. For example, one person's approach may be abstract, and he may argue that circles are better than squares. Alternatively, discuss opinions on green design, design reality shows, or traditional presentation media versus those employing electronic media.

- Give the group a single issue to debate and then divide members into two groups, each taking a different side of the argument. Allow group members enough time to organize their arguments.
- Call on a spokesperson from each side to start the debate. Position these two people standing in the center of the circle, facing each other.
- Members of either group may raise a hand to contribute to the debate. You can call on them to replace their spokesperson in the debate.

Positive Greetings. Now that the group members are acquainted, use this exercise to develop positive and personal working environments.

- Give group members time to observe each other and to consider the positive comments that could be made about their fellow participants. Members should base these comments on their interactions and experiences throughout the previous exercises.
- Group members move around and offer a greeting and a positive comment to whoever crosses their path. For example,

"Hi, I'd just like to say I thought you handled the debate really well. You were quite obviously in control of the situation." Complete this part with everyone talking at the same time.
- Stop after everyone has said something positive about all other members of the group.

Anticipating objections:

- Read the article "Lost in Space" by Warren Berger about the Chiat/Day working spaces (www.wired.com/wired/archive/7.02/chiat.html).
- Go to the website of Welcoming Workplace: Rethinking office design to enable growing numbers of older people to participate in the twenty-first century knowledge economy. Study the research findings and recommendations for workplace design (http://www.hhc.rca.ac.uk/welcomingworkplace/).
- Write down at least 10 possible objections to the Macquarie Group Limited space by Clive Wilkinson Architects that you viewed on video in Chapter 2.
- How can you respond to each of those objections in a presentation?

8 Analysis

*T*wo weeks ago the senior class had a PechaKucha thesis presentation. The opportunity arose to go before my scheduled time (that wasn't for another two hours) so I jumped the gun and went for it. Completely caught myself off guard, but I wanted to push myself out of my comfort zone. I don't know why I do these things, but the presentation ended up going pretty OK. We presented in front of our professors and guest design critics to give us feedback on our progress. I received my feedback today and it was reassuring to see that my project is going in a great direction. One comment that stood out was "your excitement is contagious." That made my day.[1]

— Kristyn Hill, interior designer

raise for work that is well done is motivating and helps you move on to tackling items that need improvement. Interim desk critiques and studio critiques of final presentations are methods used to analyze student presentations and solutions. Professional designers use similar processes to improve their presentations, identify unresolved issues, prepare documents and actions for the next phase, and follow up with the client. This is a perfect opportunity to build up project management skills.

Academic Critiques

The electrifying part of teaching design is giving support to the delivery of individual student creativity and the exhilarating results. Students must view feedback on their design presentations as feedback from a client, supervisor, or colleague just as design professionals do in practice. Students have a great potential to learn from anyone involved.

For the student and practitioner, critiques or juries occur at different phases of the design process and can be formal final design presentations or informal reviews of your work in progress. These reviews are about improving your skills and the project. The main difference for students is that their presentation will be one in a series; they will have a limited amount of time to present; and they may be graded. Design learners can gain much from the wealth of experience of both design instructors and practitioners. Think of a critique as collaboration and a chance to advance your professional development skills. Collaboration is a way to benefit from critique feedback.

The design educator is assessing your work and efforts, and like the client, is part of your project team. Team members want you to do well and are on your side. Don't consider this process as simply a chance for someone to grade your work, for it is much more than that. The important opportunities of a critique for design team members and students are:

- Showing how you have solved the design problem and met your own objectives
- Practicing oral delivery of a presentation using the vocabulary of interior design to educate and persuade clients
- Testing your ideas in a safe environment
- Enhancing your critical skills by becoming involved in the discussions
- Learning from others and viewing the work of your peers
- Receiving feedback regarding your strong points, weakness, and ways to make improvements
- Practicing how to respond to criticism using design language in support of your design solutions
- Developing time management skills
- Celebrating your accomplishments

Use these opportunities to work on and refine your professional development. In addition to learning from personal experience, you also learn from the reviews of your peers. Never be afraid to ask your audience for feedback. Their observations can help you solve problems and improve your future work. Acknowledge that you want to improve, as this is an attitude that makes it easier to accept criticism. Do not become defensive, or you risk losing the stimulation of thinking about new ideas. Instead, take out a sheet of tracing tissue and draw the suggestions given to you. Finally, record what happened during the presentation. Ask an observer or student to take notes of the review for you. Later on, reflect on the presentation and ask yourself these questions:

- What went well?
- What can I do differently?
- What did I learn from my presentation?
- What did I learn from other presentations?
- What will I incorporate into my next design project and presentation?

> ▶ "Herein lies the perfect opportunity for making the most of your design education: months of work are reduced to the fateful five minutes when you present your ideas to an audience of colleagues. First, note that this is a dress rehearsal for the rest of your life, and second, take every opportunity within the studio and beyond to get comfortable presenting ideas in front of other people. Like it or not, this will be how your life is transacted." Andrew Caruso, Gensler

> ▶ "That design thinking is expressed within the context of a project forces us to articulate a clear goal. . . . It creates natural deadlines that impose discipline and give us an opportunity to review progress, make midcourse corrections, and redirect future activity. The clarity, direction, and limits of a well-defined project are vital to sustaining a high level of creative energy." Tim Brown

Often students evaluate each other using the same criteria as an outside jury or using a point system for each task of the design process. These tasks are illustrated in Figure 8.1. It is also good practice, time permitting, that the instructor reviews the evaluation with the student before, during, and after the project presentation. Many critiques are structured in relation to the scope of services of an interior designer and are expanded to include detailed design process tasks for each phase. Following this format supports the learning of project management skills. The broad format of a point system for each task is based upon typical jury sheets used for student design competitions. The point allocation is to be determined by the design educator—a scale of 1 to 5, for instance. Remember that a design problem never has one single resolution, and the solutions presented and evaluated are how you have solved the project needs—it is what makes you distinctive.

Perhaps your school has a studio culture policy that supports a positive exchange of ideas and builds self-worth. If so, you can expect an honest critique from your instructor and visiting professionals. You should not expect a harsh critique but one that evaluates your imagination, methodology, visual and spatial literacy, absorption and synthesizing of information, collaboration and communication skills, and ability to meet deadlines, to name just a few factors. Ineffective critiques include statements directed at the person, are embarrassing, or vague. If you are told, "You are in the wrong field," "A child can do better than this," "This does not work," or "This looks like a horrible place to live," ask why. You should expect specific details about your work in order to learn and improve. Figure 8.2 illustrates some general comments you can expect to hear during a critique or see on an evaluation form. They would be accompanied with specific comments relating to your project.

> ▶ "There is nothing like focusing on the larger problems of the world to put our problems in perspective, and I suspect that once we truly engage with the world, many of the silly or self-destructive traditions of studio life—the all-nighters, the obsessions with grades, the ridiculous competition to see who will be the most original—would disappear or seem irrelevant in light of these larger purposes." Tom Fisher, dean of the College of Architecture and Landscape Architecture at the University of Minnesota

Post-Presentation Responsibilities

Act upon the critique direction and guidance related to your design project. This is the time to refine and explore your ideas or solutions and, like artists with great passion, be excited about it. Follow up on all

Figure 8.1
Design tasks. The figure can be copied to use as needed.

PROGRAMMING EVALUATION	**CONCEPTUAL DESIGN EVALUATION**	**DESIGN DEVELOPMENT EVALUATION**	**FINAL DESIGN PRESENTATION EVALUATION**
PROGRAMMING REQUIREMENTS	CONCEPTUAL DESIGN REQUIREMENTS	DESIGN DEVELOPMENT REQUIREMENTS	FINAL DESIGN PRESENTATION REQUIREMENTS
⋮	⋮	⋮	⋮

◄ 110 ►

DESIGN TASKS

PROGRAMMING	CONCEPTUAL DESIGN	DESIGN DEVELOPMENT	FINAL DESIGN PRESENTATION
Research and collect data and analysis	Preliminary furniture and/or fixture selection	Final planning concepts	Planning concepts endorse program and research data
Code issues	Preliminary color and materials	Final design concepts	Design concepts endorse programs and researched data
Prepare core plans and elevations	Preliminary ceiling design	Final furniture and/or fixture selection	Egress, fire and safety, and ADA code compliance
Visualization sketches	Preliminary lighting	Final color and materials	Furniture, fixtures, and finishes functional and suitable for use
Concept statement	Preliminary elevations	Final ceiling design	Creativeness of planning solution
Matrix and bubble diagrams	Perspective sketches	Final lighting	Rationality of planning solution
Team participation and responsibility	Preliminary budget and cost benefits	Final elevations and sections	Inventiveness of design solution
Interviews	Schematic fixture design	Perspective sketches	Practicality of design solution
Role playing	Preliminary power plan	Renderings	Inventiveness of furniture fixtures and materials
Brainstorming	Preliminary floor covering plan	Final budget and cost benefits	Practicality of furniture fixtures and materials
Synectics	Accessibility	Ability to meet schedule	Final ceiling design solution
Buzz sessions	Fire and safety	Does it communicate the concept and program	Final lighting plan solution
Dialogue groups	Mock preliminary plan check	Ability to be built	Elevations and sections
Block plans	Proper plan annotations	Solution compatible with building	Renderings
Program preparation	Ability to meet schedule	Solution ecologically responsible	Budget and cost benefits
Preparation of project schedule	Charrette		Ability to meet schedule
Ability to meet schedule	Verbal presentation		Oral presentation
			Graphic readablility, correctness, (use of scale), and clarity
			Proper labeling and keying
			Craftsmanship and neatness
			Organized presentation of materials

Programming Phase is also referred to as Strategic Planning

Conceptual Design is also referred to as Schematic Design or Preliminary Design

recommendations and prepare to discuss and review your revisions with the instructor during the next class meeting. If the critique feedback resulted from a final design submittal, make the improvements to the design project before making it part of your portfolio. These are important opportunities for learning and improvement. Act as if you are a design professional using your project management skills.

When you find it difficult to accept criticism, think of your instructor or jury as mentoring you. They are sharing experience and knowledge with you. Thank your instructor informally, outside of class, and say, "Thanks, I tried the suggestion, and it worked very well. Looking forward to showing you the revisions in class." Thank jurors and visiting professionals formally with a letter. It shows you are professional and helps build your network of contacts. For instance, the body of your letter may include:

Thank you for your feedback during my design critique. Your ideas and recommendations for the design project were a great help to me. I implemented the [state revised work] and it resulted in [state significant benefit from the change].

The professional courtesies you learn as a student should be extended to clients throughout your career by way of thank-you letters, meeting notes, and post-presentation telephone calls. All of these follow-up practices have benefits for the designer.

Thank-You Letters

Business etiquette includes sending a thank-you letter to the client within a day or two after the presentation. This letter may include the details of what will happen next, replies to questions that were unanswered in the presentation, or any follow-up information you committed to in a quick reply to the client. For example:

Dear Charles:

Thanks for a great meeting yesterday. We feel the presentation was a success, and the feedback from you and your team was valuable. We have developed a few new ideas, particularly related to the recital studios, based on the issues you raised during the meeting. We are excited to review them with you at the next presentation.

I enjoyed meeting Susan Young, and am glad to have her ideas regarding the rehearsal equipment room.

Can we schedule a meeting in a week's time? We can then prepare the revisions you and your team asked for. I will call you by the end of the week to confirm a meeting time.

Sincerely yours,

The thank you letter is a courtesy, not documentation of the presentation meeting notes.

Meeting Notes

On the contrary, the formal documentation of what occurred during the presentation is contained in the meeting notes. They include detailed comments of what was approved by the client, clarification of required revisions, and the timing and action plan for the revisions. During a presentation, usually more than one person from the design project team takes notes. Notations are also made on drawings during a presentation. As soon as possible after the presentation, all notes are collected and edited into one set of formal meeting notes. Before these notes are distributed to participants, they are reviewed and approved for content by

Figure 8.2
Critique comments. The figure can
be copied to use as needed.

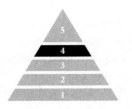

LEVELS OF
PERFORMANCE

COMMENTS
REGARDING
TASK OR
PROJECT
ASSIGNMENT

MASTERED

Work demonstrates that the design process is a complex exploration of a design problem with numerous issues interdisciplinary in nature.

Work evidences creative thinking process: research, divergent thinking, and experimentation, decision-making, application.

Highly creative use of design, composition, aesthetics, and ideas are present. Originality to space planning and graphics are exceptional.

Planning of adjacencies, circulation, and furniture placement is creative and original to design of occupancy.

Building codes are clearly implemented to occupancy, ADA accessibility is obvious. Clearances show circulation to go beyond the minimum requirements.

Furniture, finishes, and materials are appropriate, durable, functional, maintainable, and aesthetic. Materials meet code compliancy in fire retardation.

Presentation integrates media for maximum impact and clarity.

Student presents a clear, specific understanding of the competency.

High interest and excitement have led the student to reach far beyond the requirements.

EXCEEDED

Creative design and demonstrates use of imagination to design appealing spaces.

Work is very appealing, shows thinking, processing, problem solving. Codes are evident in use of circulation requirements and occupancy necessities. Design shows care of ADA regulations.

Finishes and materials are appropriate and meet code compliancy. Technical abilities are developed, content is relevant. Design composition is considered and well managed.

Student presents a clear, specific understanding of the competency.

High interest and excitement leads the student to an investigation that reaches beyond requirements.

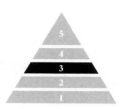

ATTAINED

Satisfactory use of composition, originality and creativity is common and needs more excitement and imagination.

Adjacencies, furniture placement, and circulation need improvement. Some areas are difficult to function in clearances and placement, some code requirements are met, and ADA regulations are partial to occupancy. Circulation is only at minimum requirements.

Furniture and materials are typical and lack aesthetic appeal. Functionality and durability is common.

Work shows some degree of success, purpose, and idea development.

Student explores options in greater detail making informed modifications to improve solution.

Apply visual and verbal communication methods in a manner that support and convey intent.

Student meets assignment expectations.

Participation, assignments, and projects meet the standard level of achievement.

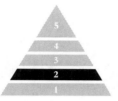

APPROACHING ATTAINMENT

Work exhibited lacks imagination and creativity. Composition is less than ordinary and shows no originality to design.

Planning lacks care of furniture placement, circulation is insufficient, and adjacencies do not meet program requirements.

Codes are not implemented well. ADA regulations are lacking for accessibility. Circulation does not meet minimum requirements. Materials are noncompliant.

Finishes are inappropriate and lack aesthetical quality. Furniture is un-proportional to space and materials are noncompliant.

Assignment has been addressed; there is a sense of effort, however ideas are underdeveloped.

Student knowledge of the topic is understood, but at minimum level of competency.

Student does most of what is required, but nothing more.

UNATTAINED

There is no evidence of imagination and creativity. Overall, design lacks originality and care to design intentions.

Solution shows no evidence of space planning. Furniture is out of scale, there is no circulation, and adjacencies are distant with no care to program requirements.

There is no evidence of code implementation and is deficient of ADA regulations.

Project demonstrates lack of exploration, is incomplete, and technique is underdeveloped. Work reveals minimal student engagement.

Student abandons options quickly preventing a coherent progression of design development.

Visual and verbal communication is basic and often lacks detail and clarity, distracting from design intent.

Student knowledge of the subject is not shown.

Projects and assignments are not executed well and are behind the standard level of achievement.

ANALYSIS

Figure 8.3
Effective feedback. The figure can be copied to use as needed.

FEEDBACK CHARACTERISTICS	DESCRIPTIVE	SPECIFIC	POSITIVE
	Tell them what you observed.	Tell them how to improve.	Begin and end with encouragement.
EFFECTIVE	The opening graphic image really captured my interest. I lost clarity when you explained the overall design concept in the opening statement.	Perhaps you could try to simplify it with a summary of the primary ideas behind the design.	The opening graphic image really captured my interest. I lost clarity when you explained the overall design concept in the opening statement. Perhaps you could try to simplify it with a summary of the primary ideas behind the design. I liked the way your illustrations reinforced the concept throughout the entire design of the space.
NOT EFFECTIVE	The opening statement was very confusing.	You need to work on your delivery.	The opening statement was very confusing. The graphics and illustrations are great.

CONSTRUCTIVE

Make suggestions for improvement.

It would be easier for me to absorb the graphic information if you would organize the presentation boards differently. Maybe you could try placing the furniture and material samples on a separate board. This one with the additional white space is very easy to associate with the floor plan. The illustration technique on the plan is divine.

The presentation boards are crowded with too much information.

SENSITIVE

Be kindhearted.

I like your line drawing technique because it is very fluid. Taking these lines to this vanishing point can perfect this patterned area of the illustration. The composition demonstrates excellent use of line to create both balance and dominance.

The perspective is wrong.

REALISTIC

Offer attainable objections.

We had a difficult time seeing and connecting to you because the podium is too high. A lavaliere microphone would be perfect in order for you to present without obstructions. You appeared very relaxed and poised while presenting.

You are too short to stand behind a podium.

Figure 8.4
Oral Presentation Evaluation Form. *(Project, C. 2008. "Presentation Evaluation Forms." Connexions, July 23, 2008.*
http://cnx.org/content/m16933/1.4/ [Derivative])

	UNATTAINED	APPROACHING ATTAINMENT	ATTAINED	EXCEEDED	MASTERED
CONTENT	1	2	3	4	5
Subject Knowledge • Organization					
Parts clearly relate to one another.					
Presentation is well organized and shows control.					
Presentation parts flow well together and have smooth transitions.					
Message is succinct but not choppy.					
Conclusion is clear.					
Presenter adheres to time schedule and includes appropriate breaks.					
Presenter demonstrates control of the audio/visual equipment.					
Presenter demonstrates competence and comfort during the presentation.					
Presenter adapts to the cultural or business concerns of the viewers by choosing details that suit their preferences.					
Group seems well rehearsed.					
Transitions from one team member to the next are smooth.					
NONVERBAL SKILLS	1	2	3	4	5
Poise • Eye Contact • Body language					
Presenter behaves like a professional and treats his or her viewers in a way that elicits professional behavior as well.					
Presenter shows personal excitement or enthusiasm for the design.					
Presenter maintains eye contact with viewers, seldom looking at notes or visuals.					
Presenter demonstrates appropriate and well-timed gestures, pauses, and fluid movements.					
Presenter's appearance is appropriate.					
Presenter displays confidence and appears relaxed.					

VERBAL SKILLS	UNATTAINED 1	APPROACHING ATTAINMENT 2	ATTAINED 3	EXCEEDED 4	MASTERED 5
Enthusiasm • Elocution					
Words are pronounced clearly without fillers and restarting sentences.					
Words are pronounced correctly.					
Viewers are able to clearly hear the presenter.					
Engaging or helpful analogies presented are persuasive to the audience.					
Presenter uses familiar, engaging language and defines any technical terms.					
Presenter demonstrates expertise by answering all questions and objections with explanation and elaboration.					
Team members work well together as a group.					
CREATIVITY	**1**	**2**	**3**	**4**	**5**
Visuals • Graphics • Storytelling					
Very original presentation of materials.					
Uses the unexpected to full advantage and captures viewers' attention.					
Illustrations and design images are explained clearly.					
Visuals are relevant, support design concept, and profive enough evidence to convince viewers.					
Overall presentation appearance is pleasing to the eye.					
Visuals are clear, contrast well with background, and easy to read and see.					
Leave-behind documents are neat and original.					
Positive comments:					
Advice for improvement:					

the persons who took the notes during the presentation and the project team leader. Often, a designer includes a sentence at the end of this letter stating, "If we do not receive a response from you within X days, we assume that the above meets with your approval." It allows the client's participants some time to review the meeting notes and comment if their understanding varies from the notes. It also allows the designer to proceed in a prescribed number of days if there is no response within the stated period. This letter outlines the agreed-upon responsibilities of both designer and client that came about as a result of the presentation and is distributed to each individual who attended the presentation.

Implementation Schedules

One of the first items Massimo Vignelli discusses with his clients after a final presentation is the implementation schedule. Two types of implementation schedules exist—project realization and presentation follow-up. A follow-up schedule sets the direction for the next steps and lists the tasks by priority. Once a list of action items, resolutions, open issues, the method for presenting design revisions, and the time schedule for completing revisions are circulated, the design team will meet on several occasions to complete their tasks. Likewise, students must do the same during the process of their design projects.

Post-Presentation Review

If you want to know about your performance, ask questions and request specific feedback. What exactly do you want to know?

- Where did the listeners become bored?
- Where did you connect with the viewers?
- Which pieces of information were clearest?

- Where did the client lose sight of the concept or description?
- Where did you have trouble speaking clearly and/or emphatically?
- Did you stay within your time limit?

Post-presentation reviews are valuable to designers and design teams in order to improve their skills and performance. During a presentation, there are areas that go well, go not so well, and simply do not work. Identification and evaluation help to generate ideas on what problematic elements to improve and how to improve them. This project management technique makes the next presentation more successful. These review meetings involve the presentation team and often a member of upper management. Students are encouraged to tape-record their critiques and then review them a few days later.

Generally a task list for a review meeting is to:

- Establish meeting goals and responsibilities of participants, identify accomplishments and problem areas, and make recommendations for improvement
- Present a summary of the project presentation
- Identify accomplishments
  - ▸ What were the greatest strengths and why
  - ▸ What went according to plan
  - ▸ Discuss and evaluate
  - ▸ Make recommendations
- Identify problems
  - ▸ What are the significant weaknesses and why
  - ▸ What did not go according to plan
  - ▸ Discuss and evaluate
  - ▸ Make recommendations

An action plan can be developed and distributed after the review meeting. Designers also find it useful to distribute a written questionnaire, as outlined above, before the meeting takes place. In that case, save discussion and evaluation for the meeting. This gives the participants time to reflect and articulate responses and consider recommendations for improvement.

Be constructive when providing feedback in both academic and professional studios. The most valuable comments provide criticism of the performance of a group or individual, not his or her personal character. Positive comments and constructive criticism offer a respectful evaluation. Beebe and Beebe categorize effective feedback as including the traits of being *descriptive, specific, positive, constructive, sensitive,* and *realistic* (Figure 8.3).[2] Always end an oral evaluation with an encouraging atmosphere and positive commentary. Figure 8.4 illustrates the evaluation categories of the presentation delivery.

The evaluation can be expanded to include considerations for group presentations. Key items to consider for group presentations are how well the team members worked together, rather than as individual presenters. This includes offering help to others in the group, contributing as needed to decision making, respecting and supporting others in the team, assuring consistency in style, and facilitating smooth transitions from one team member to the next.

▶ Designers are full of ideas; as a result, providing suggestions with your feedback is simply intuitive.

Dialogue with John R. Sadlon

Mancini Duffy, New York, New York
John R. Sadlon, Managing Principal

Q. What are some of the items you discuss with the client immediately following (or the following day/week after) a final design presentation?

A. Immediately after a final design presentation, it's good practice to follow up with a thank-you message to the client. The purpose is two-fold: to express your respect and appreciation for their time and consideration of your presentation, and to restate the primary message of your design solution. This simple gesture will help to keep your presentation fresh in the client's mind, especially if you were competing with other designers. As appropriate, the message may also express an interest in continuing a dialogue about the project with the client. You may inquire about scheduling a second meeting and/or interview.

Whenever possible, an effort should be made to solicit feedback from the client (and any other individuals who may have been present in the room), specifically regarding the quality of your presentation. Was your message clearly articulated? Did your message resonate with the client? Did your design solution address each of the client's primary concerns? In what ways could your presentation have been more effective? The answers to these questions will help you understand not only how effective your preparations were for this presentation, but will also help you to prepare more effectively for future opportunities. This is important whether or not your design is ultimately approved. Presentation skills should always be considered as evolutionary, responding to the changing needs of your audience on a case-by-case basis.[3]

Idea Exchange

- Listen to this point of view, "The Lost Art of Crit que" by Aaron Irizarry. http://vimeo.com/14021248. 10 August 2010.
- "The Art Critique: Its History, Theories, and Practices," by Chris Mansour, *What is Critique?* is an all day symposium that consists of panel discussions with artists, critics, teachers, and students city-wide that investigates the role that art critiques and criticism play in art production. It was held on 20 November 2010. http://newyork.platypus1917.org/what-is-critique-symposium-video-documents/.

Create Experience

Critique Group Charrette.

The goal of this assignment is to develop your critical thinking skills and support your analysis with specific facts to improve each other's work in progress and final presentations.

- Present your work in front of a group of your peers.
- They will analyze your work and your presentation both orally and in writing.
- Provide constructive criticism of each other's work.

Use the evaluation forms and techniques from this chapter and guidelines from the instructor, or develop evaluation instruments of your own. This must be conducted as a team meeting review not as a design jury review.

9 Media

*S*carpa probably had synesthesia [an unusual condition in which normally distinct senses or perceptions overlap—e.g., the association of a particular flavor with a specific color, or of a certain sound with an abstract shape]. For him, the purpose of a drawing was not just to depict what any human could see, but somehow to convey the totality of what we feel. Students in his class would make drawings in which, of course, the trees were green and the bricks were red, and so on. But Scarpa did not like this. He was not interested in a drawing as a representation of a real building; for him, the drawing should express some essence—some perceptual presence of an architectural idea—rather than just pretending to be a photographic substitute.[1]

— Marco Frascari

The choice of media should also express the essence of your design idea to motivate the client to commit by making a decision. Visuals that convey credibility build trust. Choose media to optimize and influence trust and emotion. Use the medium, or combination of media, to best demonstrate the design character and spirit of the interior to the client. Today, this is accomplished by a comprehensive knowledge of both the technique of hand and that of electronic media.

Media Engagement

For the "Make it Work, Engineering Possibilities 2009" show at New York's Center for Architecture, an engineering firm exhibited an Impact Project. It used the well-known Xbox to present an easy and familiar way to experience the project computer models. But then again, by the time you are reading this, Kinect for Xbox has already eliminated the need for a controller device. Should all PowerPoint presentations bring into play a PechaKucha format? Will Prezi do away with PowerPoint? Will virtual user experiences such as Second Life be used to present designs and eliminate the need for a designer to personally facilitate a presentation? Or perhaps designers will be creating our visual graphics for a more immersive virtual reality experience such as Cave Automatic Virtual Environment (CAVE). Our presentation rooms will be the theater for adventure to experience a simulated world. Exciting possibilities.

Doubtless, all of the elements of the presentation visuals must engage the viewer in ways to diminish any blocks, barriers, or fears. Your primary persuasion objective at this point is to create visual elements that demonstrate how you have fulfilled the aspirations of the client. Furthermore, the objectives are to engage viewers to persuade them to support their own causes. Clearly identify all of your persuasion objectives,

precisely articulate them, and then select the appropriate techniques from your unique set of presentation skills. The basic methods are numerous, combinations are never-ending, and the media is continually evolving.

Yet, you are not restricted to using either computer programs or hand skills. The thoughtful choice of media is an opportunity to engage both the client and yourself. Persuasive visuals of any kind are an opportunity to be used to inspire the client to take action on the design solution that, after all, they requested. When Bryant Rousseau asked Sir Peter Cook about the drawbacks of computers and imagination in design, Cook responded,

> Some of the product suffers from its ease of production. That you can press a few buttons and something quite dreamy and slithery comes out the other end, but you don't have to stop and think about it. There's a certain sort of product you get from having to really worry something, from having to turn a corner and fight your way to it. Whereas if the digits just do it for you, the facility can sometimes act against the intensity of thinking whilst you're fighting your way through.[2]

In order to optimize engagement with the presentation visuals, designers learn and use basic skills. Freehand drawing, technical drawing, digital drawing, hand and computer illustration, composition, and artistry are perfected in order to understand what is the best medium to apply to a presentation. The different media and methods are selected based on several criteria including:

▶ "I've noticed the computer sometimes leads to rather bland decision making; now anybody can do a wobbly, blobby building."
Sir Peter Cook

- The unique attributes of the media
- Skill level with the media
- Visual appeal
- Clarity and coherence in communicating an understanding of the design solution
- Communication needs for the phase of the design process (preliminary ideas, final presentations, detailed construction drawings)

By far, the most important factor to consider is how best to explain the design concept in a preliminary or final presentation. Visually, it is important to have a complementary relationship between the media and the design concept to reinforce understanding and engagement for a client.

Basic production methods to create visuals are completed with a computer, by hand, or a combination of both. Those visuals may be in a loose or tight drawing and presentation style. The presentation is shown to the client using digital media, paper media, or a combination of the two. Examples of these production methods are illustrated in Figure 9.1 through 9.8 and Color Plates 28 through 34.

▶ "For 50 years, my tool has been a Faber-Castell 2b with an eraser and a sheet of white paper." Matteo Thun, architect, interior designer

▶ "Mastering a 3-D program is not enough. . . . There are things that are harder to learn and yet more important. I'm talking about . . . the sense for compositions, colors, and an overall balance in the scene. If you want to be good in this field, first grab a camera instead of the mouse and keyboard and go out some place and practice." Viktor Fretyán, architect and visualization artist, Budapest, Hungary

▶ "I always showed interest in traditional art forms. In fact, from the early age, my biggest interest was drawing, painting, and clay modeling. What I regret is that after discovering the computer slowly I stopped drawing and painting, so lately I'm trying to work more on my skills . . . but as always time is the worst enemy. In my case the traditional background helps me as I look at my works more in the 'artistic' way than strictly technical and correct." Zoran Gorski (Kizo), Arscom Studio, Croatia

Don't be afraid to add a twist to the media selection. Imagine using the style and technique of Color Plate 32 if you plan to present a modern historic interior to "Mad Men" type, Madison Avenue ad executives. It would be a refreshing surprise.

Touch media is the material samples for the project as illustrated in Figure 9.9 and 9.10. They are presented as loose media, adhered to a board surface, or digitized. Digital images are printed as well as inserted into an electronic presentation such as PowerPoint or Prezi.

◀ 125 ▶

▶ "In the design process I don't use the computer at all—only for the execution phases." Markus Benesch

Media Layering

A client without a design background or knowledge of architectural drawing methods will not easily relate the visual elements to your narrative. The viewer needs more than a well-arranged collection of data

Figure 9.1
This group of photorealistic renderings by Roberto De Angelis are an example of tight style and computer-generated graphics and most definitely have a clinical feeling. These illustrations represent a final design presentation (a). People give an illustration a relationship of scale and soften the mechanical nature of the rendering style. One-point perspectives tend to be static; therefore, adding foreground devices such as a large plant or people will guide the viewer's eye through the space (b). Immersive views show more detail of an interior space (c). This illustration clearly shows the space available to accommodate additional seating or wheelchairs and is an important feature to include in the oral delivery along with the visual design details (d). *(Sant' Alessandro Clinic, Rome, Italy. The project remodel of the interior public zones by architect Franco Bernardini)*

Figure 9.2
Photorealistic rendering by Roberto De Angelis is a tight style, computer-generated graphic. Apartment entry, Rome, Italy (a), apartment living room (b), apartment dining room (c), apartment kitchen (d). *(Design by architect Franco Bernardini. Video animation with 3-D studio max at http://archiviz.wordpress.com/2010/04/18/appartamento-quartiere-aurelio-roma-architetto-franco-bernardini-visual-design-roberto-de-angelis/)*

Figure 9.3
Preliminary concept study of living room. Freehand-style illustration edited with computer graphics program by Lisa Mitchell, interiorstylestudio, Beaconsfield, England.

Figure 9.4
Perspective elevation study. Freehand-style illustration edited with computer graphics program by Lisa Mitchell, interiorstylestudio, Beaconsfield, England.

and visuals with text. Well-implemented presentation media are easy to move through and understand. "Information layering could be carried out by simple, cross-media . . . or complex method . . . with each medium supporting or illustrating the message by the other medium or media,"[3] as described by Kwee. Figure 9.11 illustrates these prototypes. He also explains that you must be careful that the visual information presented allows the viewer to explore the material, evaluate the design solution, and generate his or her own opinion and decision. This means giving clients enough time to look at each visual while you pause quietly for a few moments. Their eyes will return to you when they have finished their initial exploration. Time restricted, linear presentations,

such as singular video formats, do not allow this to happen. Neither does the spoken narrative. Therefore, you also need a complementary relationship among the media used.

Layering of visual information is a strategy used to build a clear, visual conversation with a distinctive progression of media incorporation. That does not mean to incorporate a great deal of text. Dr. Stephen Kosslyn, psychologist, and Robert Lane, presentation design consultant, state,

> Text and pictures . . . compete for perceptual and cognitive resources when juxtaposed—you can focus on one

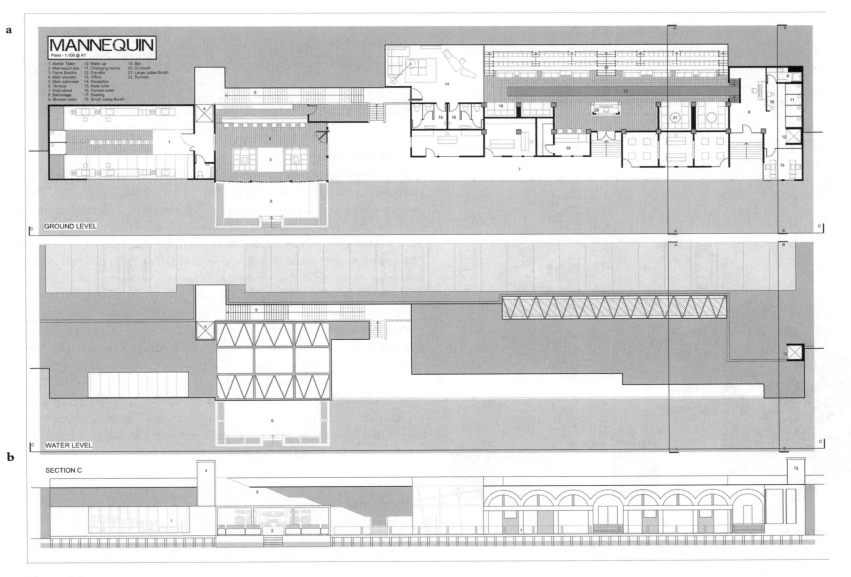

Figure 9.5
CAD drawings for final presentation (a). Floor plan of two levels with simple color and tone designations (b). Section drawing showing interior space.
Mannequin Bar by Thomas Watts, Interior Design.

or the other, but not both at the same time. Viewers must try to read the text, look at the picture, and pay attention to the speaker's words, all in a short time span. Most of us fail to do all three and either ignore the text and listen to the speaker, or try and read the text and miss the speaker's words.[4]

Use labels, headlines, captions, and short phrases as needed, but a presentation is not like reading a book with images.

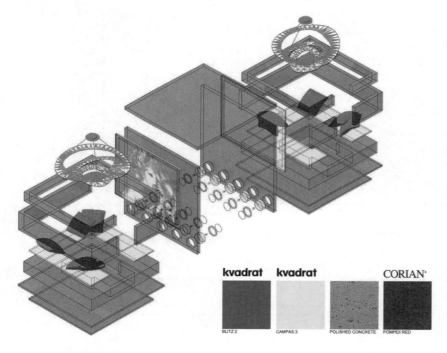

kvadrat   kvadrat   CORIAN®

BLITZ 2   CAMPAS 3   POLISHED CONCRETE   POMPEII RED

Figure 9.6
Detailed expanded or exploded view and material samples of Fame Booth to show the relationships between the parts of the whole design feature. Mannequin Bar by Thomas Watts, Interior Design.

> ► "To avoid having the text conflict with the picture, or the text conflict with the speaker's verbal stream, the solution is obvious. Simply dump the text and use a full screen visual." Dr. Stephen Kosslyn, psychologist, and Robert Lane, presentation design consultant

Multilayering

Borrowing from the Kwee prototypes, the multilayered design presentation is very similar to the concept of grouping related information. This is not a new technique employed by designers in presenting information. Rather, it encourages the use of multiple media within the groups. For instance, include an animation or manufacturer's video clip of how a product works because it offers additional information not evident on the plan or image of the product. A video is one example of this, as is incorporation of models, mock-ups, various views, larger detailed views, or zooming in to show detail. Say, "Let me show you what I mean," when shifting to detail with alternate media. Do not use multiple media simply for the sake of using more than one medium. Systematically, you show the client what the design solution is with visuals along with the verbal story. If the additional media type will strengthen and clarify a design feature, help the viewer make a connection to your concepts, or make ideas concrete, it is to your benefit to use it. Nonetheless, be sure it complements other media. Still photorealistic illustrations along with animation is illustrated in Figure 9.12.

> ► "So it has the obligation to be both Beethoven's Fifth Symphony, some of it, but also to be background music sometimes. And that's a great balance." Paul Goldberger, author and architecture critic for *The New Yorker*

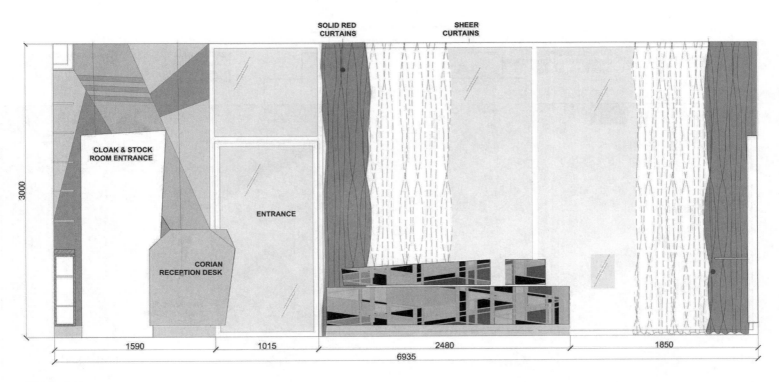

SOLID RED CURTAINS

SHEER CURTAINS

CLOAK & STOCK ROOM ENTRANCE

3000

ENTRANCE

CORIAN RECEPTION DESK

1590   1015   2480   1850

6935

Figure 9.7
Elevations of significant interior walls are illustrated to present highly detailed room elements. Elevation CAD drawing for concept presentation of Peter Mark salon by Garry Cohn.

Animation

Animation of interior space is a method to immerse the client in the spatial experience—a virtual tour of an interior. This type of technology is primarily utilized by developers, resort property owners, and real estate agents as a sales and promotional tool. Regardless of promotional possibilities, the virtual reality animations give viewers the feeling of moving about inside the space. These animations can be as simple as a 3-D panoramic view or 3-D interactive walk through or as complicated as a 3-D stereoscopic architectural animation requiring 3-D glasses for viewing. The 3-D panoramic views allow the viewer to look at a full 360-degree scene and zoom in or out. These animations are movies and can be incorporated into a computer slide presentation (Figure 9.13).

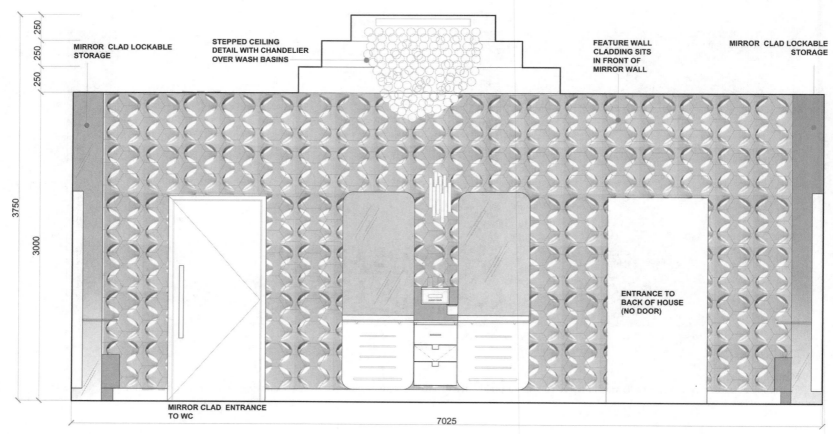

250 250 250 250 250

3750

3000

MIRROR CLAD LOCKABLE STORAGE

STEPPED CEILING DETAIL WITH CHANDELIER OVER WASH BASINS

FEATURE WALL CLADDING SITS IN FRONT OF MIRROR WALL

MIRROR CLAD LOCKABLE STORAGE

ENTRANCE TO BACK OF HOUSE (NO DOOR)

MIRROR CLAD ENTRANCE TO WC

7025

Figure 9.8
Elevation CAD drawings of feature wall for concept presentation of Peter Mark salon by Garry Cohn.

Media–Generated Realities

We can entertain our clients and help them evaluate design with virtual reality, augmented reality, and mixed reality applications. You have seen augmented reality (AR) show the possibilities for combined real world/ virtual world in architecture and interior design solutions. For instance, the research by Bauhaus-Universität Weimar, Spatial Augmented Reality for Architecture (sARc) in 2007, termed on-site Trompe l'oeil, whereby photorealistic images of the proposed design and material of

Figure 9.9
Material boards along with reference imagery are presented at various stages of a project for client approval. Laguna Day Spa by Julie Paille, Paille Interior Design.

an interior surface could be experienced virtually on the actual spatial surface. The goal is to simulate an atmosphere in actual space to assist in design decision making. Choose your jargon term—technotecture or heterarchitecture—for the next generation digital design tool kit. Dr. Hartmut Seichter, architect and software engineer, helped create Sketchand+, a collaborative augmented reality application for sketching on a digitizer tablet and then placing the virtual image on a site plan model. Sofia Lagerkvist, Charlotte von der Lancken and Anna Lindgren of Front, inspired by their fascination with magic, produced Sketch furniture (Figure 9.14). Design process sketches, drawn in the air, appear through technology, and more. Watch the entertaining process at this link www.designfront.org/category.php?id=81&product=92. The Museo dell'Ara Pacis (Rome, Italy) by architect Richard Meier is the building featured in a graduate thesis multimedia project by Sorin Voicu (Figure 9.15). The movie demonstrates how he imagines using augmented reality to change the way we learn—about architecture, for instance. Enjoy the video at this link www.soryn.it/PORTFOLIO/PROJECTS/2009_Augmented_Reality.html.

▶ "Today it's not enough to just know the programs! You have to do more than that! One of my professors at university used to tell me 'good enough is not good nor enough' and if I think of my work I find this saying very true." Viktor Fretyán, architect and visualization artist, Budapest, Hungary

▶ Animated motion—move into space walking forward. Do not move out of space as if you are walking backward.

Figure 9.10
Material samples as loose format. Images (a). Material samples arranged in vignette
(b). Digital material samples as loose format (c). Digital material samples as loose
format with text (d). *(Courtesy of Shaw Industries Contract Carpets)*

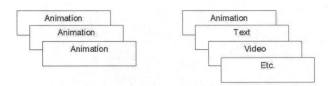

Figure 1. Examples of Simple and Cross Media Layering

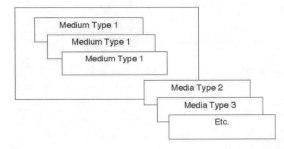

Figure 2. *An Example of Complex Layering*

a

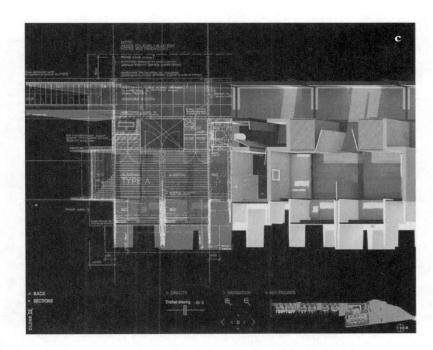

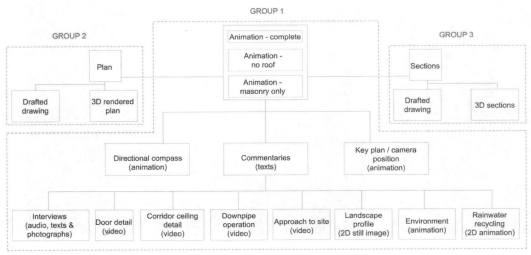

Figure 5. Hierarchy and Layering in the Illustrative Prototype

b

Figure 9.11
Kwee's basic concept is that each medium supports the other (a). Kwee's prototype shows three groups with connected layers to provide in depth understanding of information presented (b). Kwee's prototype showing the use of Group 2 and 3 layering (c).

MEDIA

Figure 9.12
Peter Guthrie, architect and visualization artist, believes every image must portray the built form in the most elegant and efficient way (a). A progression is established simulating the experience of walking through each gallery space (b). Lighting techniques emphasize the window and skylight features as well as creating dramatic shapes of light (c). Realistic depiction of the sculpture encourages viewer interaction (d). Equal emphasis is placed on the spatial design and its contents. *(Scarpa's Hall in the Museo Canoviano designed by Carlo Scarpa. Visualization by Perter Guthrie. Video can be incorporated into the presentation. Visualization and animation by Peter Guthrie, Falun, Sweden, of the Museo Canoviano designed by Carlo Scarpa, architect. View the movie at http://vimeo.com/298070)*

Figure 9.13
Virtual reality animations are immersive viewer experiences and give the effect of moving about inside the space. Animation of the Renaissance created by Pure. *(www.purerender.com/gallery)*

Regardless of the method you use to create the visuals for your presentation, a basic understanding of visual composition is required in order to perfect your artistry. Computer programs are tools, as are pencils, paint, and markers. It comes as no surprise that the most successful artists, including illustrators, photographers, and painters, have a great understanding of the dynamics of three-dimensional design. You will do well if you look beyond the characteristics of the media and instead approach visual presentation with holistic awareness. Artist Bertrand Benoit shares his experience:

> I do have a relatively strong—and much older—drawing background, but I think my comparatively recent photography background is much more crucial to making my 3-D work better. It helps you to know how far you can push some effects . . . without making an image photographically implausible. I think it's no coincidence that many of the best Archviz artists, people like Peter Guthrie, are also excellent photographers in their own right." [5]

right" ◄ 137 ►

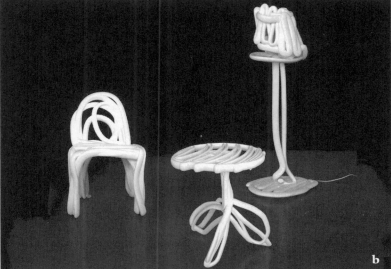

Figure 9.14
Sketch furniture by Front. Motion Capture translates sketch gestures into 3-D files as Front uses the technique to record the tip of a pen while they draw furniture in the air (a). The 3-D files go through a process of Rapid Prototyping where a laser beam builds the file in layers within a liquid plastic that is hardened by the laser beam (b).

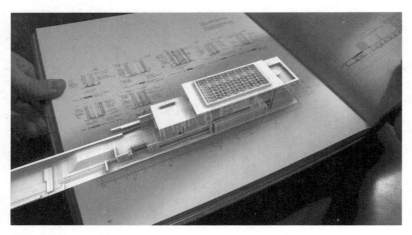

Figure 9.15
Graduate Thesis in "Computer Graphics and Multimedia Design" by Sorin Voicu. Faculty of Architecture "Valle Giulia," University of Rome "La Sapienza." Autodesk 3ds Max Design, Adobe After Effects, PFTrack, Mocha, Adobe Photoshop, and Sony Vegas is the software used.

Media Musings

Most all designers embrace new technology and apply its many forms to their daily tasks and client responsibilities. As you explore media as a means of communicating your art, please your hands and your eyes. Media should encourage involvement.

> Since he began practicing . . . the tools of his profession have changed, particularly in the past ten years. "It's much more exciting," he says. "Computers have liberated us from boxes and have allowed more sculptural architecture to be built. Technology has enabled us to produce designs and working drawings that we couldn't have produced before." He adds, "Today I'm much freer, more experienced, and able to create new and exciting designs as never before." What have we yet to see in architecture? "Floating pavilions—non-earthbound, that move through the air."[6]
>
> —Peter Marino

Today, designers look on with awe when presented a hand-illustrated design vision or handcrafted model; only ten years ago, a computer-generated image created the same response. Digital graphics could become extinct some day. Or are we so glued to virtual reality that it interferes with our ability to perceive the actual reality? We design for human beings, not machines, and our presentations ought to be a bit more human—to create an effect and to inspire. Our environment is still built with our hands. Ponder these writings by Tod Williams and Billie Tsien, architects (TWBTA), written more than a decade ago:

> Slowly, the tools of the hand disappear. In the United States, the practice of architecture has come to rely on the computer. In offices, the word efficiency is always mentioned, and in design schools, the capability to create and rotate complex forms in space is lauded. So, with surprising speed, the tools of the hand are becoming extinct.
>
> This is a lamentation for lost tools and a quiet manifesto describing our desire for slowness. We write not in opposition to computers—in fact we are in the midst of bringing them into our studio—but rather it is a discussion about the importance of slowness. We write in support of slowness.

Our desire to continue to use the tools of the hand, even as we may begin to use the computer, has to do with their connection to our bodies. Buildings are still constructed with hands, and it seems that the hand still knows best what the hand is capable of doing. As our hands move, we have the time to think and to observe our actions."[7]

—*Slowness*, Tod Williams and Billie Tsien, architects

Although Williams and Tsien continue to draw by hand, the office of TWBTA uses computers. Octavia Giovannini-Torelli elaborates on their case for slowness, saying,

> Renderings usually have evidence of the hand, and a lot of attention is paid to the materials represented in the renderings. The idea of the hand and the work of the hand are ever present in our work. We never want presentation materials to look too slick or manicured! We are constantly evolving with the requests of the clients and the need for projects to be represented in unique and individual ways.[8]

Sounds very much like the way Scarpa approached design—materials in relationship to the human. The evolution of graphic communication techniques is just as enigmatic as the character of architect Carlo Scarpa. He began his career as a painter, product designer, and interior designer.

In writing the subheading *Slowness of Perception,* Williams and Tsien point out that computer-generated presentation methods, such as a "fly-through," are cold "machine-like lenses . . . that follow a too logical sequence of movement. A human eye scans panoramically, and then suddenly focuses on a tiny point. You see the ocean, and then you see a grain of oddly colored sand."[9]

▶ "New inventions which will enable us to move about in space in new ways and at new speeds will bring about a new reality. The static architecture of the Egyptian pyramids has been superseded—our architecture revolves, swims, flies. We are approaching the state of floating in air and swinging like a pendulum. I want to help discover and mould the form of this reality." El Lissitzky, artist, engineer, architect

Dialogue with Peter Joehnk

JOI-Design, Hamburg, Germany
Peter Joehnk, and Corinna Kretschmar-Joehnk, Principals

Q. Can you give a description of the particular methods that you have used for different project presentations?

A. Our standard method is to prepare all the drawings (colored) in DWG files, find mood pictures (abstract themes and design solutions from others), get the local flavor, choose colors and materials from the library . . . and finally compile the whole thing into a PowerPoint presentation.

Q. How has technology changed how you make presentations to clients? Can you comment on the success of digital versus traditional media? Is it a success? How do you combine the different digital formats? Do you find clients are more receptive to one format over another? Do you use traditional media or computer-generated presentations? Do you present actual finish material samples when presenting with electronic media?

A. [W]e do the presentation with three media: we use a beamer presentation, the participants get printed hand-outs of the presentation, and we do big prints of the main drawings, which get glued on hard paper, as well as sample boards with original materials for a haptic experience. Colors and materials can be shown digitally for a general overview, but they also have to be presented physically. The presentation with computer and beamer has developed a lot in the last years and the software to produce the presentation is developing quickly . . . we try to follow.

Q. What about the use of 3-D video animations? Please describe all digital formats you use in design presentations.

A. We have a film for our office presentation, but we don't do 3-D video animations, except if the client specifically requires them and pays separately. Anyway, all different "production methods" then get integrated in a "classic" PowerPoint presentation.

Q. Most of us are eager to know the latest trends for presentation techniques. What is the new direction for your firm? For you as a designer?

A. The development of 3-D presentation, by walking individually through our created spaces, will probably be the next step, but for the moment, we keep it simple.[10]

Idea Exchange

- Architectural Record: Channels, Firms in Focus.
- Firms in Focus: Richard Meier, Pt. 1 and 2. A Visit to Meier's Model Gallery. http://video.construction.com/?fr_story=c071a34214efbbafb9ea490b30bda74624fb9e27&rf=sitemap. http://video.construction.com/?fr_story=c071a34214efbbafb9ea490b30bda74624fb9e27&rf=sitemap.
- Jacques Herzog of Herzog & de Meuron, Transforming Tate Modern: The architect's vision. 20.11.2008. http://channel.tate.org.uk/media/26518590001.
- Panorama of interior created by PressEnter Design, Poland. http://pressenterdesign.com/pano/mtm.swf.
- Photorealistic visualization of a reception area modeled with 3ds Max, V-Ray, and Photoshop created by Luis Cardoso, 3-D Senior Visualizer, London, UK. http://www.evermotion.org/portfolio/show/reception/727357/2842.
- Interior 3-D animation created with 3ds Max 2010 and V-Ray 1.5 sp4 produced by Bertrand Benoit. http://vimeo.com/9682327.
- 3ds Max Design interior design animation by Roberto De Angelis. Design by architect Franco Bernardini. www.youtube.com/watch?v=kMr8uZ8atFE. (Images at http://archiviz.wordpress.com/2010/04/18/appartamento-quartiere-aurelio-roma-architetto-franco-bernardini-visual-design-roberto-de-angelis/.) www.youtube.com/watch?v=ZzjB8d8Auyw&feature=related.
- Home interior 3-D animation using V-Ray created by Aldekas Studio. www.youtube.com/watch?v=d_t19RA2luM&feature=related.
- Two Nest Village conceptual presentation animation video by OFIS Arhitekti. http://vimeo.com/10403050.

Create Experience

Make your design presentation look great. Using an existing project, create a new presentation specifically tailored for your audience. Focus on the quality of graphics and information while determining the best medium or combination of media to communicate the design concept effectively.

10 Professionalism

*D*uring the years of cold and shortages, Gertrude Stein and Alice B. Toklas became friends with a neighbor . . . named Pierre Balmain, with a taste for antiques and a natural bent for designing women's clothes. In fact, he made with his own hands heavy tweeds and warm garments for Gertrude and Alice to wear during the hard winters. Now he has opened a shop in Paris. At his first showing to the Press, Gertrude and Alice arrived with their huge dog, Basket. Gertrude in a tweed skirt, an old cinnamon-colored sack, and Panama hat, looked like Corot's self-portrait. Alice, in a long Chinese garment of bright colors with a funny flowered toque, had overtones of the Widow Twankey. Gertrude, seeing the world of fashion assembled, whispered, "Little do they know that we are the only people here dressed by Balmain, and it's just as well for him that they don't!"[1]

— Cecil Beaton (1904–1980), English photographer and designer

Creative types are often expected to dress differently, and Stein and Toklas certainly embraced change through a culture of creative dressing. Today artistic individuals appear in the workplace wearing vintage Balmain and most certainly have a flair for the bold and eccentric! The beauty of the design business culture is the freedom to dress corporate or dress creative. Much of dressing smart, professional, or creative depends on how you want to be seen and, of course, the work culture of the client or your employer. Without a doubt, it is important to be yourself and feel comfortable while understanding the difference between what is appropriate while you work and what is appropriate for a client meeting.

> ▶ In 1954, famed costume designer Edith Head (1897–1981) was delighted to be awarded an Oscar for her contribution to the film *Roman Holiday*. "I'm going to take it home," she declared to reporters "and design a dress for it!"

A Finely Tailored Presenter

Interior designers, fashion designers, graphic designers, art directors, product designers, costume designers, set designers, and architects tend to have a unique work look. Although architectural firms seem to be the most conservative type, most design businesses opt for a variation of formal business dress for client meetings. A fun fact is that countless designers and architects plan their attire to fuse seamlessly with their presentation. The clients' culture also has its own unique work look. When asked if she had any fashion confessions to share, costume designer Jenny Beavan replied, "I have absolutely no interest in fashion or clothing unless I am using clothes to tell a character's story. Then I become *very* interested in whatever is appropriate to that character."[2]

Does your appearance reflect passion and purpose? Can you go to a meeting and look like a refined professional? Clean, classic looks for professional settings do not have to be overly traditional. As a designer, you should look current, relevant, and professional because it reflects your talent. Looking and feeling your best builds confidence; furthermore, a confident presence is noticeable to your viewers. Fashion designer Michael Kors says, "Audrey Hepburn has projected an image of style and not of fashion." Sophisticated and gracious are always in style.

When it comes to personal style, wardrobe and image consultants are of the same opinion regarding the practical basics of choosing the right garments—details count. These details include garment quality, fit, comfort, sight, and sound. If your clothes look sloppy, so do you. Sloppy, tight, or short do not equate with creative dressing. On the contrary, it can be quite distracting and does not truly represent the culture of the design industry nor does it convey professionalism. Make sure your clothes are wrinkle and stain free and in excellent condition. Do not wear clothing that does not fit well—too tight or too baggy. Do not wear clothing that is transparent or revealing or shows undergarments. Do not wear any item that makes noise when you move. Excellent grooming is basic—polished shoes, clean hair, neat nails. Women should not overdo it with accessories; rather, keep it simple and understated. In other words, do not combine large jewelry around your face or wear jewelry that makes noise. No overpowering cologne or perfume. Pulling all of it together tells others that you are polite, considerate, and respectful enough to not offend others with your choices.

> ▶ "Our company guidelines regarding appropriate business attire for a presentation are formal business or personal interpretation." Massimo Vignelli, Vignelli Associates

Look the part by choosing appropriate clothing for your role. Additionally, dress one step more formal than your viewers, as it helps your credibility. Professional speakers dress to keep attention focused on their face—at most, choose only one focal point for each part of your body. Do not wear any item if you are not comfortable in it or it detracts from your ability to concentrate or perform. During a presentation, you want the viewers to focus on your skills and contribution, not on your clothing.

Use your dress to promote your business image and your personal image. This includes having consideration for the client's image and your employer's image. Formal business attire is normally appropriate in certain industries such as law and finance because it projects a stable and credible image. That includes the basics, such as a pair of black pants, a dark pantsuit, a button-down collared shirt, and a pair of classic polished dark shoes (socks should match your trousers). In a business casual setting, men may prefer a sports jacket, shirt, and tie instead of a shirt and tie only. The tie is optional, but a dress shirt and tailored trousers are required.

Take your cues from the very first meeting with the client. Dress formally for that meeting and pay close attention to the unstated dress code. You can then adjust your clothing for the next meeting. Jack Nicholson noticed the *visual barometer* of the set design by Beth Rubino for *Something's Gotta Give*:

> "Nancy (Meyers, director, writer, and producer) wanted a house that looked decorated . . . so we created something wonderful and homey, but chilling"—a feeling Nicholson picked up on when he first visited the set. "During wardrobe fittings," recalls Meyers, "I could see Jack was going toward shorts and polo shirts. So I said, 'Let's take a look at the house where you'll be spending time,' and as soon as we got there, he said, 'Oh, I get it. No shorts.' "[3]

No one wants to be without personal style; however, it should enhance your professional presence. Lisa Kline, a New York wardrobe stylist, says, "When in doubt, go for sleek and sophisticated." Dress appropriately for the design industry, and that can include looking chic.

▶ "I always like to present a cohesive vision of the office. Mostly the attire is black and white." Vicente Wolf, Vicente Wolf Associates

Poise and Style

Understanding the client brand and image is quite important; nonetheless, an honest evaluation of your personal image deserves as much attention. How do others perceive you in and out of your business environment? How you identify yourself in the design business is how others will identify and value you. You have to pay attention to what is happening around you and regularly evaluate both how you fit in and how you wish to evolve in the design business culture. Position and represent yourself well in order to achieve your goals.

By extension, John R. Sadlon, managing principal at Mancini Duffy, believes it is important for designers to distinguish themselves from the rest of the crowd. He states,

> It is also essential to develop your personal style of delivering a formal message. This process begins with an understanding of your characteristics and personality, and ideally, it allows your unique attributes to shine through in your presentation style. This process often requires discipline to focus your patterns of speech and behavior in order to achieve your desired outcome. The focus should

be on your self-expression as a means to connect with your client/audience, and to quickly establish a level of trust in you based on the knowledge and creative approach that distinguishes you from everyone else.[4]

Charismatic leaders use appearance, body language, and words to align themselves with their goals and, these aspects of self-presentation, if used sincerely, can effectively motivate others. Charisma is developed through perfecting your communication techniques. It has to do with both verbal and nonverbal social skills. In his book, *The Charisma Quotient*, Dr. Ronald E. Riggio, Ph.D., describes personal charisma as having six fundamental qualities:

- *Emotional expressiveness*: a spontaneous and genuine way of expressing feelings that has an effect on others
- *Emotional sensitivity*: making a connection to others by responding to their feelings
- *Emotional control*: the demonstration of emotion is synchronized and managed
- *Social expressiveness*: words and expression are engaging and powerful
- *Social sensitivity*: the ability to synchronize with others in social interactions
- *Social control*: the ability to carry oneself with poise and grace and fit in any social setting

When a speaker has truly charismatic behavior, the results are emotional contagion.[5] Frank Bernieri, Ph.D., observed that individuals with high rapport also demonstrate high expressiveness. He believes synchrony is connected to charisma and says, "It's all about timing, repetition and rhythmic cadence of their speech, raising amplitude at key points."[6] Those features of speech can capture the rapt attention of listeners.

Additionally, use of personal space, facial expressions, spoken language, and hand and body gestures are all different ways of communicating. When nonverbal communications do not match our words, the message can be confusing. Shifting posture, smiling, and using eye gestures will have a positive influence on your words. In general, flowing, smooth curvilinear gestures give the impression of friendliness and sensitivity; straight and angular gestures are sensed as commanding or forceful. The Center for Nonverbal Studies in Spokane, Washington, developed *The Nonverbal Dictionary of Gestures, Signs, and Body Language Cues*. The material is interesting to explore and useful in practicing your art of nonverbal communication. These are defined at the website: http://center-for-nonverbal-studies.org. However, be aware that body language is not universal, and you should take cultural differences into account. Gestures used by someone in the United States can frequently have a different meaning when used in Japan, for instance. Japanese listeners are taught to focus on a speaker's neck in order to avoid eye contact, while in the United States, listeners are encouraged to gaze into a speaker's eyes.[7]

In all cases, your attitude must *confirm* the message of your words. Would you trust any words if the speaker's physical attitude suggests something to the contrary? Vital information is communicated in a face-to-face exchange through:

- Tone of voice
- Facial expression
- Pupil activity
- Body carriage, proximity, and extremity orientation
- Gaze projection
- Breathing style/rhythm
- Hand position, formation, and behavior

Often, people respond more to nonverbal clues than to the actual words spoken. Study your body language and make certain to align it with the message you wish to communicate.

Equally important is to become attuned to the flow of your biorhythms in order to perform at the best of your ability. This requires well-synchronized internal cycles to function both physiologically and psychologically. It helps us to maintain our attention and motivation. Most of us are familiar with the circadian rhythms of the body regarding sleep rhythms set to the day. The body also has ultradian rhythms, of short duration, occurring throughout the day. According to Dr. Roseanne Armitage, many of our body and brain functions are set for tasks in ninety-minute cycles.[8] Armitage recommends that we need mental breaks between those cycles to enhance concentration.

Likewise, a few simple rules for business meeting etiquette, mentioned here and in Chapter 6, should be followed for any type of meeting or presentation. During formal or informal meetings, it is important for you to demonstrate professionalism:

- Prepare an agenda ahead of time and distribute it to the participants before the meeting so they may also prepare for the meeting.
- Arrive a few minutes early for the meeting and start on time.
- Turn off your cell phone before entering the meeting room.
- Be prepared with a writing tablet and pen in order to take notes.
- Participate in the conversations without interrupting others.
- Remain calm and diplomatic at all times.
- Address the chair of the meeting when following formal meeting protocol.
- Be attentive and listen carefully to what others are saying. Never create side conversations or cross talk. Remember that meeting conversations are confidential, as a rule.
- Never leave a meeting early.

- Be courteous and professional by thanking the participants and, in particular, the chair of the meeting.
- Follow up with action items to all in attendance and request meeting feedback if you are the chair of the meeting.

This is easy because it is simple courtesy and manners and shows your respect for your business and others.

> ▶ "Design is a way of life. It is not a profession, it is not a tool, it is a philosophy. You use it to guide a way of life." Tony Chi

Confidence

Most communication and publicity experts agree that appearance shapes an initial impression. It is a substantial nonverbal cue about your image. Your business dress must reflect you, your goals, your employer, your profession, and the occasion. Dress poise and style also project confidence. When you have mastered any specific task or subject matter confidence occurs naturally. Knowing your presentation material thoroughly results in confidence. David Greusel, AIA, explains it this way: "This means knowing more, much more, about the subject than you will ever have to say."[9] It is not merely memorizing your lines.

Consequently, when you are completely focused on the presentation, you are in the flow of your task. Aim for a relaxed concentration during the presentation and completely remove any issues unrelated to the presentation from your thoughts. Simultaneously, be attentive to what is occurring around you during the presentation in order to respond. Your confidence naturally improves when you are completely immersed in a task.

In his study of the psychology of creativity and creative flow, Mihaly Csikszentmihalyi stresses the importance of focus. Csikszentmihalyi explains that the nervous system can only process about 110 bits of information per second. When you are completely focused on the presentation, you will not process any other outside information. In other words, if you let personal concerns, your hair, or meeting your next deadline into your thoughts, you are not immersed in the presentation. If your mind is on these distractions, it will erode your confidence and weaken your ability to perform. Csikszentmihalyi found that when you are in a state of flow, specific conditions seem to be present.

> There's this focus that, once it becomes intense, leads to a sense of ecstasy, a sense of clarity, you know exactly what you want to do from one moment to the other, you get immediate feedback. You know that what you need to do is possible to do, even though difficult, and sense of time disappears, you forget yourself, you feel part of something larger. And once those conditions are present, what you are doing becomes worth doing for its own sake.[10]

Therefore, find your confidence in your consistently successful accomplishments and know what your abilities and strengths are. Keep building those strengths and abilities in order to establish your reputation and credibility. This can enhance your recognition as an expert in the field. That leads to building self-confidence. Create a presence of honesty, empathy, and mutual respect.

In reality, you are delivering a performance and creating an experience for the viewers the minute you step in front of a group of people to address them. Live it and be it, says Los Angeles image expert Judy Jernudd. Smile; make contact with your eyes to connect with others. A genuine sparkle in your eye reflects happiness and invites everyone else to be part of the project. Make eye contact with the individual viewers

for a few seconds, have open gestures, and speak clearly. Remember this: "By this time you know you have a good idea; you just don't yet know how good it is."[11]

> ▶ "Think of the presentation as meeting with people individually. This will give you the confidence and you will be able to connect." Vivek Singh, MBA

Protocol

Once you have mastered the other skills in this chapter, you are ready to study business etiquette for your international contacts and global travels. Knowing the acceptable way to conduct business with a client from a different cultural background will lead you to successful interactions. This section is a simple introduction to the subject of protocol. Protocol consultants can assist with all aspects of business communication and offer training or tips on negotiating practices and business entertaining worldwide.

Gift-giving is one of many cultural items to consider and prepare for. For instance, if you're doing business with a Japanese client, it may be a formal procedure. Symbolism and ceremony are significant in Japan and the Pacific Rim countries. The gift exchange shows you respect and appreciate the client relationship. When a designer receives a gift, it is the client's way of expressing gratitude and acknowledging the efforts of a refined presentation. Regardless of the gifts given to clients, don't be surprised if you receive a very generous gift in return. A Southern California design firm gave California wines to a Japanese client in Hawaii. In kind, they brought a lavish traditional Hawaiian feast on their next visit to California. Similarly, a Chinese host will delight the presenter with a time-honored banquet like the lavish Hawaiian feast after a presentation.

A note of caution for a gift leave-behind: a gift with a prominent company logo displayed is perfectly acceptable for a client in the United States, for instance, but not in Spain, Portugal, or Greece. In China, historically, a business gift is considered a bribe.

It is very important to understand the culture and personalities of your clients to determine the appropriate way to show appreciation. This includes gifts, dress, greetings, gestures, physical contact, and, yes, even eye contact. For instance, refined business attire is expected in Buenos Aires. In addition to facts, personal feelings are a strong factor for the Chinese in accepting a proposal. However, facts outweigh feelings in Austria; Austrian women do not traditionally shake hands, and Austrians are offended if you speak with your hands in your pockets.

Additional resources regarding business protocol for international clients are *World Wise: What to Know Before You Go* by Lanie Denslow, *Kiss, Bow, or Shake Hands* by Terri Morrison and Wayne A. Conaway, *Global Etiquette Guide* series by Dean Foster, ediplomat.com, and Executive Planet.com.

Throughout the pages of this story about design and presentation, both practitioners and experts are shown weaving a powerful tale, expressing the heart, soul, love, and pride of their design arts experience. Design is personal in both expression and experience. You have a unique voice—connect to others with your passion for design. Massimo Vignelli sums it up simply, "Act responsibly with professional knowledge, and confidence comes by itself."[12] He goes on to say that a presenter should possess the skills of "knowledge and charm—firmness and flexibility."[13] Vicente Wolf adds to the list of needed talents "salesmanship, a logical mind, a warm personality, and uncompromising belief in the client's design."[14]

Dialogue with Peter Joehnk

JOI-Design
Peter Joehnk and Corinna Kretschmar-Joehnk, Principals

Q. How do you gain the confidence to present a design? What hints or tips can you provide for designers to build their confidence in presenting a design? Is this confidence tied to the design, and how successful do you as a designer feel in solving the design problem?

A. If a designer is confident with the content of the presentation and likes his own design (and why not!), then they should be confident enough to make the presentation. Sometimes there are circumstances that can make me less confident—such as not enough space in the room, a bad projector, clients writing e-mails in the presentation, or even worse, picking up phone calls or talking during the presentation.

Q. What qualities and skills should a presenter possess?

A. The universal quality is respect for the audience and the knowledge of the designer's "authority" on the subject. It is important for the audience to believe in what the presenter says.[15]

Idea Exchange

- Advice from professional designers at Project Connect: http://www.projectconnectdpe.org/vidcat/videos/advice1.html. http://www.projectconnectdpe.org/vidcat/videos/advice2.html.
- Itay Talgam: "Lead Like The Great Conductors." www.ted.com/talks/itay_talgam_lead_like_the_great_conductors.html.
- "Mihaly Csikszentmihalyi on Flow." www.ted.com/talks/mihaly_csikszentmihalyi_on_flow.html.
- Richard St. John: "Success is a Continuous Journey." www.ted.com/talks/richard_st_john_success_is_a_continuous_journey.html.
- "Richard St. John's 8 secrets of success." www.ted.com/talks/richard_st_john_s_8_secrets_of_success.html.

Create Experience

Attributes. This exercise will help you evaluate your personal behaviors and perfect them into a polished personal brand. Keep a journal and review it weekly. Record:

- Your accountability and reliability
- Your enthusiasm and passion for your specific responsibilities
- Why the above is important to you
- Your strengths and weaknesses
- What you love to do and why you love doing it
- What can make you more valuable to an employer or client
- How often you recognize a need and initiate performing a task and how often you wait to be asked
- Awareness of your influence on situations, and whether it is positive or negative
- Awareness of what is happening around you
- Image, posture, body language, verbal communication skills. Do they reflect you and your intentions?

Define and develop your network:

- Whom you have worked with
- Whom you socialize with
- Who are the key people—past, present, and future—who can help you reach your goals

Personal Journal

Watch the video "Ken Carbone is Curiously Curious" at DesignIntelligence (http://www.di.net/videos/ken_carbone_curiously_curious/). Keep a journal to record your thoughts, feelings, and inspirations from the world around you.

Endnotes

Introduction

1. Moeller, Martin, "The Tell-Tale Drawing: An Interview with Marco Frascari," *Blueprints* 25, no. 3 (Summer 2007), www.nbm.org/about-us/publications/blueprints/the-tell-tale-drawing.html.

2. http://www.charlierose.com/view/interview/11125#frame_top.

3. Talgam, Itay, "Itay Talgam: Lead Like The Great Conductors." Filmed July 2009. TED video, 20:52. Posted October 2009, www.ted.com/talks/itay_talgam_lead_like_the_great _conductors.html.

Chapter 1

1. Goldberger, Paul, "Spiffing Up the Gray Lady," *The New Yorker,* January 7, 2002, www.newyorker.com/archive/2002/01/07/020107ta_talk_goldberger.

2. Giovannoni, Stefano. Bisazza, Designers, "Stefano Giovannoni," Video Interview, accessed 20 August 2009, www.bisazza.com.

3. Peter Joehnk (Principal, JOI-Design), interview by Christina Scalise, electronic questionnaire, June 18, 2010.

4. Mau, Bruce, "Design Collaborations," *Shaw Contract Group,* www.shawcontractgroup.com/Html/DesignCollaborations.

5. Ibid.

6. Serraino, Pierluigi, "Fulton Residence, Hollywood, California. Rodney Walker," in *Julius Shulman, Modernism Rediscovered*, text by Pierluigi Serraino, 043. Taschen, 2009.

7. Owen, Charles, "Design Thinking: Notes on Its Nature and Use," *Design Research Quarterly* 1, 2 (December 2006): 25, www.drsq.org/issues/drq2-1.pdf.

8. Fuller, Edmund, *2500 Anecdotes For All Occasions* (New York, NY: Avenel Books, 1978), 221.

9. McClain, Gary, *Presentations: Proven Techniques for Creating Presentations That Get Results*, 2nd ed. (Avon, MA: Adams Media, 2007), 52.

10. "What We Do: Design Research Studio," Mayo Clinic, 2010, http://centerforinnovation.mayo.edu/sparc.html.

11. Navarro, Antonio Pérez. Design Hotels, Made By Originals, The Design Hotels Collection, "Antonio Pérez Navarro," accessed 20 August 2009, www.designhotels.com.

12. Tischler, Linda, "Marcel Wanders Designs Miami's Mondrian," *Fast Company Magazine Online,* October 01, 2008, www.fastcompany.com/magazine/129/moooi-fabulous.html?page=0%2C4.

13. Griskevicius, Vladas; Shiota, Michelle N.; and Nowlis, Stephen M. "The Many Shades of Rose-Colored Glasses: An Evolutionary Approach to the Influence of Different Positive Emotions," *Journal of Consumer Research* 37 (August 2010).

14. Ibid.

15. Paul Conner, CEO of Emotive Analytics, e-mail message to author, May 4 2010.

16. Pignon-Ernest, Ernest, "Cinderella: The scenery; a picture book," *Les Ballets de Monte-Carlo,* (April 3, 1999), http://www.balletsdemontecarlo.com/programmes_en/synopsis/cendrillon.html.

17. Peter Joehnk (Principal, JOI-Design), interview by Christina Scalise, electronic questionnaire, June 18, 2010.

Marginal Notes

Page 9: Gehry, Frank, "Frank Gehry asks 'Then what?'" Filmed February 2002. TED video, 22:04. Posted January 2008, www.ted.com/talks/lang/eng/frank_gehry_asks_then_what.html.

Page 12: Mackey, Sally, ed. *Practical Theatre: A post-16 approach* (England: Stanley Thornes Publishers, 1997).

Chapter 2

1. "AD 100: José E. Solís Betancourt," *Architectural Digest,* 2010, www.architecturaldigest.com/architects/100/solis_betancourt/solis_betancourt_profile.

2. "SANAA: "Kazuyo Sejima and Ryue Nishizawa; New Museum of Contemporary Art," arc*space* (December 01, 2003), www.arcspace.com/architects/ sejima_nishizawa/new_museum/.

3. Alan Dandron (Principal, Mancini Duffy), interview by Christina Scalise, electronic questionnaire, June 03, 2010.

4. Herman Miller, "Three-Dimensional Branding: Using Space as a Medium for the Message," Herman Miller, Inc. (2007), www.hermanmiller.com/MarketFacingTech/hmc/research_summaries/pdfs/wp_3D_Branding.pdf.

5. Pine, B. Joseph, II and Gilmore, James H, "Welcome to the Experience Economy," *Harvard Business Review* (July–August 1998).

6. Serraino, Pierluigi, *Julius Schulman: Modernism Rediscovered*, Koln, Germany: Taschen, 2009.

7. Gabellini Sheppard, "Vera Wang Boutique," Gabellini Associates, accessed August 15, 2011, www.gabelliniassociates.com/index.php/Projects/retail/vera-wang-boutique-5h.html.

8. Claudio Silvestrin Architects, Projects, Interiors, "Princi Bakery Duomo, Milan," Accessed 20 August 2009, www.claudiosilvestrin.com.

9. Haldeman, Peter, "Steve Wynn Expands His Empire with a Dazzling Las Vegas," *Architectural Digest* (April 2009), www.architecturaldigest.com/homes/hotels/2009/04/hotels_encore?printable=true#ixzz0wVCNvd9f.

10. Walker, Cassie, "Wish You Were Here: SLDesign and B. R. Guest bring barefoot flair to the Postcard Inn in St. Petersberg, Florida," *Interior Design* (January 01, 2010), www.interiordesign.net/article/ca6715275.html.

11. AAI, "Hitachi Global Storage Technologies International Headquarters," AAI (2009), www.aaidesign.com/services/interior-architecture/portfolio.php?id=102.

12. Contemporist Blog; "Artis Capital Management Office Interior by Rottet Studio," blog entry by Dave, April 15, 2010, www.contemporist.com/2010/04/15/artis-capital-management-office-interior-by-rottet-studio/.

13. Ibid.

14. Ibid.

15. Vicente Wolf (Vicente Wolf Associates), interview by Christina Scalise, electronic questionnaire, April 09, 2010.

16. Claudio Silvestrin Architects, Philosophy-Books, Aphorisms by C. Silvestrin, Accessed 20 August 2009, www.claudiosilvestrin.com.

17. Chi, Tony, Tony Chi and Associates, "About Us," Accessed 12 April 2010, www.tonychi.com.

18. Gladwell, Malcolm, *Blink: The Power of Thinking Without Thinking* (New York: Little, Brown and Company, 2005), 272.

19. "AD 100: Samuel Botero," *Architectural Digest,* 2010, www.architecturaldigest.com/architects/100/samuel_botero/samuel_botero_profile.

20. Ibid.

21. John R. Sadlon (Managing Principal, Mancini Duffy), interview by Christina Scalise, electronic questionnaire, June 03, 2010.

Marginal Note

Page 24: Interview by Christina Scalise, electronic questionnaire, June 03, 2010.

Chapter 3

1. Frank, Michael, "Palladian Spirit. A Florida Residence Fit For an Ambassador," *Architectural Digest* (December 2005), www.architecturaldigest.com/architects/100/axel_vervoordt/vervoordt_article_122005?currentPage=1.

2. Israel, Toby, "Design Psychology 101: Some Place Like Home; Matching People and Place Through Design Psychology," *Perspective* (Spring 2001), www.designpsychology.net/pdf/handout_perspective%20article.pdf.

3. The Design & Emotion Society, 2006, www.designandemotion.org.

4. Shedroff, Nathan, "Design: A Better Path to Innovation," *Interactions: Emerging Approaches to Research and Design Practice* 15, no. 6 (November–December 2008).

5. Straczynski, Stacy, "Designer Perspectives: Future Corporate Design Trends," *Contract Design* (May 19, 2010), www.contractdesign.com/contract/design/Designer-Perspective-1925.shtml.

Marginal Notes

Page 34: Simpson, Scott, "Eight Steps to Better Communications," *DesignIntelligence* (May 15 2003), www.di.net/articles/archive/2179/.

Page 37: Suqi, Rima, "Women in Design: Victoria Hagan," *Elle Décor,* www.elledecor.com/decorating/articles/victoria-hagan-interior-design.

Page 41: Interview by Christina Scalise, electronic questionnaire, April 09, 2010.

Chapter 4

1. Ivy, Robert, "Power Player: The Many Lives of Bill Lacy," *Architectural Record* (2009), http://archrecord.construction.com/features/interviews/0801lacy/0801lacy-2.asp.

2. Schnaper, Harry, "Interviews: Harry Schnaper," *Architectural Digest*, 03:09, Accessed 20 August 2010, www.architecturaldigest.com/video?videoID=33051595001.

3. Caan, Shashi, "New York School of Interior Design Graduation Address," May 19, 2010, www.nysid.edu/NetCommunity/Page.aspx?pid=562.

4. Ivy, Robert, "Power Player: The Many Lives of Bill Lacy," *Architectural Record* (2009), http://archrecord.construction.com/features/interviews/0801lacy/0801lacy-3.asp.

5. Wong, Gillian, "Designer Perspectives: Christian Hogue Dishes on Marketing Strategies for Solo Architects and Small Firms," *Contract Design* (April 26, 2010), www.contractdesign.com/contract/design/Designer-Perspective-1675.shtml.

6. Brown, Tim, *Change By Design. How Design Thinking Transforms Organizations and Inspires Innovation* (New York: HarperCollins Publishers, 2009), 23.

7. NCIDQ Glossary of Terms, www.ncidq.org/AboutUs/AboutInterior Design/DefinitionofInteriorDesign.aspx (accessed 10 April 2010).

8. Pressman, Andrew, "It's A Very Good Time To Develop Your Firm's Collaboration Skills," *Architectural Record* (April 2009), http://archrecord.construction.com/practice/firmCulture/0904collaboration-1.asp.

9. Alan Dandron (Principal, Mancini Duffy), interview by Christina Scalise, electronic questionnaire, June 03, 2010.

10. Peter Joehnk (Principal, JOI-Design), interview by Christina Scalise, electronic questionnaire, June 18, 2010.

Marginal Notes

Page 48: Niemeyer, Oscar, "Oscar Niemeyer 101," *Motherboard*, VBS.TV, May 18, 2009, www.vbs.tv/watch/motherboard/oscar-niemeyer-101.

Page 50: Shoemaker Rauen, Stacy, "Meet the Minds Behind Restaurant Design—Glen Coben," *Hospitality Design* (May 17, 2010), www.hospitalitydesign.com/hospitalitydesign/projects/Meet-the-Minds-Behin-1806.shtml.

Page 51: *Moeller, Martin,* "The Tell-Tale Drawing, An Interview with Marco Frascari," *Blueprints* 25, no. 3 (Summer 2007), www.nbm.org/about-us/publications/blueprints/the-tell-tale-drawing.html.

Page 52: Interview by Christina Scalise, electronic questionnaire, June 03, 2010.

Page 54: Shoemaker Rauen, Stacy, "Meet the Minds Behind Restaurant Design—Glen Coben," *Hospitality Design* (May 17, 2010), www.hospitalitydesign.com/hospitalitydesign/projects/Meet-the-Minds-Behin-1806.shtml.

Page 57: "Design-Designer Profiles: Caleb Mulvena and Colin Brice; Perspectives; Mapos, LLC," Contract: Inspiring Commercial Design Solutions (September 11, 2009), www.contractdesign.com/contract/design/Perspectives-Mapos-815.shtml.

Page 57: www.twbta.com/cup_print.php?p=wc&id=2204.

Page 59: Interview by Christina Scalise, electronic questionnaire, June 03, 2010.

Page 59: http://blog.uxusdesign.com/press/.

Chapter 5

1. Shoemaker Rauen, Stacy, "Meet the Minds Behind Restaurant Design—Glen Coben," *Hospitality Design* (May 17, 2010), www.hospitality design.com/hospitalitydesign/projects/Meet-the-Minds-Behin-1806.shtml.

2. Alan Dandron (Principal, Mancini Duffy), interview by Christina Scalise, electronic questionnaire, June 03, 2010.

3. Ibid.

4. Vicente Wolf (Vicente Wolf Associates), interview by Christina Scalise, electronic questionnaire, April 09, 2010.

5. John R. Sadlon (Managing Principal, Mancini Duffy), interview by Christina Scalise, electronic questionnaire, June 03, 2010.

6. Van Duysen, Rineke, "Going for Baroque," *Interior Design* (January 01, 2007), www.interiordesign.net/article/CA6411101.html.

7. John R. Sadlon (Managing Principal, Mancini Duffy), interview by Christina Scalise, electronic questionnaire, June 03, 2010.

8. Peter Joehnk (Principal, JOI-Design), interview by Christina Scalise, electronic questionnaire, June 18, 2010.

9. Brown, Tim, *Change By Design. How Design Thinking Transforms Organizations and Inspires Innovation* (New York: HarperCollins Publishers, 2009), 126.

10. John R. Sadlon (Managing Principal, Mancini Duffy), interview by Christina Scalise, electronic questionnaire, June 03, 2010.

11. Brown, Tim, *Change By Design. How Design Thinking Transforms Organizations and Inspires Innovation* (New York: HarperCollins Publishers, 2009), 126.

12. Alan Dandron (Principal, Mancini Duffy), interview by Christina Scalise, electronic questionnaire, June 03, 2010.

13. John R. Sadlon (Managing Principal, Mancini Duffy), interview by Christina Scalise, electronic questionnaire, June 03, 2010.

14. Ibid.

Marginal Notes

Page 65: Interview by Christina Scalise, electronic questionnaire, June 18, 2010.

Page 67: Han, Qin, "Giving Research a Design Twist," *Design Studies, Design Thinking in Practice*, Design Studies at Dundee (August 16, 2010), http://designstudies2010.wordpress.com/course-notes/design-research/as-designers-we-are-equipped-with-wonderful-talents-and-techniques-%e2%80%93-that-is-visualising-and-making-things-we-are-trained-to-make-images-animations-or-objects-the-evoke-emotions-and-intera/ (accessed August 2010).

Page 73: Rich, Carrie R., and Matthew J. DeGeeter, "Designing for Health: Research-Based Client Communication," *Contract* (May 24, 2010), www.contractdesign.com/contract/design/Designing-for-Health-1961.shtml.

Page 77: Interview by Christina Scalise, electronic questionnaire, June 18, 2010.

Page 77: "Designer Perspectives: Q&A with Lauren Rottet, FAIA, IIDA," Design, Designer Profiles, *Contract Magazine*, July 06, 2011, www.contractdesign.com/contract/Designer-Perspective-5586.shtml.

Chapter 6

1. Adams, Sean, "Designers; Q&A: Worst Speaking Experiences; Kathy McCoy," *Step Inside Design Magazine* (January 2009), www.stepinside design.com/STEPMagazine/Article/28927/index.html.

2. Peter Joehnk (Principal, JOI-Design), interview by Christina Scalise, electronic questionnaire, June 18, 2010.

3. Elkus Manfredi Architects, Montage Retail Furniture Shop, Boston, Massachusetts.

Marginal Notes

Page 90: Marcel Wanders, "Superior Interiors," *Financial Times* (May 2003), www.marcelwanders.nl/new-pages/us-quotes-new.html.

Page 91: Caruso, Andrew, "The $100,000 Question," *Design Intelligence* (November 5, 2009), www.di.net/articles/archive/the_100000 _question/.

Page 92: Greusel, David, "The Five Es of Effective Presentation Delivery," *AIA Best Practices* (September 03, 2006, revised December 2006).

Page 93: Interview by Christina Scalise, electronic questionnaire, June 18, 2010.

Chapter 7

1. Chi, Tony, "Design Giants: Tony Chi," Interior Design TV, May 03, 2010, www.interiordesign.net/video/Design_Giants/4426-Design_Giants _Tony_Chi.php?intref=sr.

2. Brand, Jay L., "Are Gen-Y's Brains 'Modular' Or 'Unconscious'?," *Haworth: Generations White Paper* (April 2009), http://www.haworth.com/en-us/ Knowledge/Workplace-Library/Documents/Are-Gen-Y-Brains.pdf.

3. Scher, Paula, *Make it Bigger* (New York: Princeton Architectural Press, 2005), 161.

4. Chan, Peter Kwok and Sanders, Elizabeth B., "Exploring, Interpreting, and Applying Emotional-Driven Design in Brand Identity Development: A Design Student Case Study" (2007). Peter Kwok Chan, The Ohio State University, USA.

5. Massimo Vignelli (Vignelli Associates), interview by Christina Scalise, electronic questionnaire, May 25, 2010.

6. Lowry, Vicky, "Women in Design: Annabelle Selldorf," www.ellede cor.com/decorating/articles/women-design-annabelle-selldorf.

7. "AD 100: Samuel Botero," *Architectural Digest,* 2010, www.architec turaldigest.com/architects/100/samuel_botero/samuel_botero_profile.

8. Massimo Vignelli (Vignelli Associates), interview by Christina Scalise, electronic questionnaire, May 25, 2010.

9. Ibid.

10. "ASID Code of Ethics & Professional Conduct," Adopted by the National Board August 2006, accessed April 10, 2010, www.asid.org/ about/ethics.

11. Simpson, Scott, "Eight Steps to Better Communications," *Design Intellegence* (May 15, 2003), www.di.net/articles/archive/2179/.

12. Brown, Tim, *Change By Design. How Design Thinking Transforms Organizations and Inspires Innovation* (New York: HarperCollins Publishers, 2009).

13. Peter Joehnk (Principal, JOI-Design), interview by Christina Scalise, electronic questionnaire, June 18, 2010.

Marginal Notes

Page 98: Suqi, Rima, "Women in Design: Victoria Hagan," www.elle decor.com/decorating/articles/victoria-hagan-interior-design.

Page 98: "Design-Designer Profiles: Caleb Mulvena and Colin Brice; Perspectives; Mapos, LLC," Contract: Inspiring Commercial Design Solutions (September 11, 2009), www.contractdesign.com/contract/design/Perspectives-Mapos-815.shtml.

Page 99: "Design-Designer Profiles: Perspectives; Arik Levy," Contract: Inspiring Commercial Design Solutions (August 10, 2009), www.contractdesign.com/contract/design /Perspectives-Arik-L-812.shtml.

Page 99: Interview by Christina Scalise, electronic questionnaire, April 09, 2010.

Page 101: Interview by Christina Scalise, electronic questionnaire, May 25, 2010.

Page 103: Shoemaker Rauen, Stacy, "Meet the Minds Behind Restaurant Design—Richard McCormack," *Hospitality Design* (July 7, 2010), www.hospitalitydesign.com/hospitalitydesign/projects/Meet-the-Minds-Behin-2155.shtml.

Page 103: Simpson, Scott, "Eight Steps to Better Communications," *DesignIntellegence* (May 15, 2003), www.di.net/articles/archive/2179/.

Page 103: Caan, Shashi, "On Collaboration," *Contract Design Magazine* (October 2002), 84.

Chapter 8

1. Hill, Kristyn, Syracuse University Interior Design 2010 Graduate Blog, March 23, 2010, http://kristynhill.tumblr.com/page/2.

2. Beebe, Steven A., & Beebe, Susan J., *Public Speaking: An Audience-Centered Approach*, 7th Edition (Boston, MA: Allyn & Bacon, 2009), 83.

3. John R. Sadlon (Managing Principal, Mancini Duffy), interview by Christina Scalise, electronic questionnaire, June 03, 2010.

Marginal Notes

Page 109: Caruso, Andrew, "The $100,000 Question," *Design Intelligence* (November 5, 2009), www.di.net/articles/archive/the_100000_question/.

Page 109: Kellog, Clark, "Focus on the Future: Learning from Studio," Design Futures Council, *DesignIntelligence, Knowledge Reports* (January 2006).

Page 109: Brown, Tim, *Change By Design. How Design Thinking Transforms Organizations and Inspires Innovation* (New York: HarperCollins Publishers, 2009), 21.

Chapter 9

1. *Moeller, Martin,* "The Tell-Tale Drawing: An Interview with Marco Frascari," *Blueprints* 25, no. 3 (Summer 2007), www.nbm.org/about-us/publications/blueprints/the-tell-tale-drawing.html.

2. Rousseau, Bryant, "The ArchRecord Interview: Sir Peter Cook," *Architectural Record* (2010), http://archrecord.construction.com/features/interviews/0711petercook/0711Petercook-1.asp.

3. Kwee, Verdy, "Architectural Presentation for Precedent-Based Learning," presented at the 3rd International ASCAAD Conference on *Em'body'ing Virtual Architecture,* Alexandria, Egypt.

4. Kosslyn, Stephen, and Robert Lane, "Show Me! What Brain Research Says About Visuals and PowerPoint," Indezine.com (February 2009), www.indezine.com/articles/whatbrainresearchsays01.html.

5. Architectural Visualization Blog; "Interview with Bertrand Benoit," blog entry by Ron Bekerman, July 25, 2010, www.ronenbekerman.com/3d-artist-interview-bertrand-benoit/.

6. *Architectural Digest,* "The International Directory of Interior Designers and Architects: AD 100; Peter Marino," *Architectural Digest* (revised January

08, 2009), www.architecturaldigest.com/architects/100/peter_marino/peter_marino_profile.

7. www.twbta.com/cup_print.php?p=wc&id=2204.

8. Octavia Giovannini-Torelli, e-mail message to Christina Scalise, May 11, 2010.

9. www.twbta.com/cup_print.php?p=wc&id=2204.

10. Peter Joehnk (Principal, JOI-Design), interview by Christina Scalise, electronic questionnaire, June 18, 2010.

Marginal Notes

Page 124: Rousseau, Bryant, "The ArchRecord Interview: Sir Peter Cook," *Architectural Record* (2010), http://archrecord.construction.com/features/interviews/0711petercook/0711Petercook-1.asp.

Page 125: Villeroy & Boch, Signs of Character, Creatives in Dialogue Edition 1.

Page 125: The Vizdepot, "Artist Interview: Viktor Fretyán," The Vizdepot (May 16, 2010), www.vizdepot.com/forums/articles.php?action=viewarticle&artid=97).

Page 125: Ron Bekerman, "Interview with Zoran Gorski (Kizo)" (July 25, 2010), www.ronenbekerman.com/3d-artist-interview-zoran-gorski-kizo/.

Page 125: Gumus, Hazal, "Markus Benesch Interview" (March 2007), www.designophy.com/interview/article.php?UIN=1000000008&sec=interview.

Page 130: Kosslyn, Stephen, and Robert Lane, "Show Me! What Brain Research Says About Visuals and Powerpoint," Indezine.com (February 2009), www.indezine.com/articles/whatbrainresearchsays01.html.

Page 130: Paul Goldberger, Author, and Architecture Critic for *The New Yorker*. Rose, Charlie, "Paul Goldberger Interview" (December 30, 2009), www.charlierose.com/view/interview/10787#frame_top.

Page 133: 3DTotal, "An Interview with Viktor Fretyan," 3DTotal Artist Interviews, www.3dtotal.com/pages/interviews/viktor_fretyan/viktor_fretyan_01.php.

Page 139: Lissitzky-Kuppers, Sophie, and Aldwinckle, H., translator, *El Lissitzky: Life, Letters, Texts*, Thames & Hudson Ltd; London, Reissue edition (Oct 1968).

Chapter 10

1. Beaton, Cecil and Buckle, Richard, *Self Portrait with Friends: The Selected Diaries of Cecil Beaton, 1926–1974* (Times Books, 1979), 164.

2. "Dress Code: Jenny Beavan, Costume Designer," *The Independent, May 20, 2010,* www.independent.co.uk/life-style/fashion/features/dress-code-jenny-beavan-costume-designer-1978427.html.

3. Collins, Nancy, "Setting the Scene for Romance in the Hamptons," *Architectural Digest* (July 2007), www.architecturaldigest.com/homes/spaces/2007/07/somethingsgottagive_article#ixzz0t7oMdmWr.

4. John R. Sadlon (Managing Principal, Mancini Duffy), interview by Christina Scalise, electronic questionnaire, June 03, 2010.

5. Cherulnik, Paul D., Kristina A. Donley, Tay Sha R. Wiewel, and Susan R. Miller, "Charisma Is Contagious: The Effect of Leaders' Charisma on Observers' Affect," *Journal of Applied Social Psychology* 31, no. 10 (July 31, 2006): 2149–2159, www3.interscience.wiley.com/journal/119017631.

6. Greer, Mark, "The Science of Savoir Faire," *Monitor on Psychology* 36, no. 1 (January 2005): 28, www.apa.org/monitor/jan05/savoir.aspx.

7. The Center for Nonverbal Studies, accessed April 10, 2010, http://center-for-nonverbal-studies.org /eyecon.htm.

8. Marano, Hara Estroff, "Biorhythms: Get in Step," *Psychology Today* (April 28, 2004), www.psychologytoday.com/articles/200404/biorhythms-get-in-step.

9. Gruesel, David, *Architect's Essentials of Presentation Skills* (Indianapolis: Wiley 2002).

10. Csikszentmihalyi, Mihaly, "Mihaly Csikszentmihalyi on Flow," filmed February 2004, TED video, 18:59, Posted October 2008, www.ted.com/talks/mihaly_csikszentmihalyi_on_flow.html.

11. Brown, Tim, *Change By Design. How Design Thinking Transforms Organizations and Inspires Innovation* (New York: HarperCollins Publishers, 2009), 107.

12. Massimo Vignelli (Vignelli Associates), interview by Christina Scalise, electronic questionnaire, May 25, 2010.

13. Ibid.

14. Vicente Wolf (Vicente Wolf Associates), interview by Christina Scalise, electronic questionnaire, April 09, 2010.

15. Peter Joehnk (Principal, JOI-Design), interview by Christina Scalise, electronic questionnaire, June 18, 2010.

Marginal Notes

Page 144: http://theoscarsite.com/1953.htm.

Page 144: Interview by Christina Scalise, electronic questionnaire, May 25, 2010.

Page 145: Interview by Christina Scalise, electronic questionnaire, April 09, 2010.

Page 147: Chi, Tony, "Design Giants: Tony Chi," Interior Design TV, May 03, 2010, www.interiordesign.net/video/Design_Giants/4426 Design_Giants_Tony_Chi.php?intref=sr.

Index